JeaNeOLOGY

Crafty ways to reinvent your old blues

Nancy Flynn
Edited by Karen Macklin

First published in 2007 by
Zest Books, an imprint of Orange Avenue Publishing
35 Stillman Street, Suite 121, San Francisco, CA 94107
www.zestbooks.net

Created and produced by Zest Books, San Francisco, CA
© 2007 by Orange Avenue Publishing LLC
Photographs © 2007 by Peter Honig
Illustrations © 2007 by Roxy Baer-Block

Text set in Eureka Sans; accent text set in Arial Black; title text set in Baveuse.

Library of Congress Control Number: 2006934915
ISBN-13: 978-0-9772660-3-6
ISBN-10: 0-9772660-3-6

CREDITS

EDITORIAL DIRECTOR: Karen Macklin
CREATIVE DIRECTOR: Hallie Warshaw
WRITER: Nancy Flynn
EDITOR: Karen Macklin
PHOTOGRAPHER: Peter Honig
ILLUSTRATOR: Roxy Baer-Block
COVER MODEL: Brooke Fraser
GRAPHIC DESIGNERS: Tanya Napier and Cari McLaughlin
PRODUCTION ARTIST: Cari McLaughlin

Distributed by Publishers Group West

Printed in China.
First printing, 2007
10 9 8 7 6 5 4 3 2 1

TaBLe of Contents

INTRODUCTION

Jeans are a girl's best friend. Your favorite pair never lets you down and can make you feel pretty on even the ugliest of days. Jeans are simply perfect for everything — dressing up, dressing down, or just plain lounging around. And while everyone already knows that jeans make great pants, *Jeaneology* will show you they also make great skirts … and key chains and coasters and pillows and purses. Have a beat-up pair of tapered blues that needs new life? Turn them into funky flares. Have a pair too tattered for patching? Refashion them into a belt and matching hair band. Just like blue jean styles, cuts, and washes, the options for re-creating your blues are endless — and *Jeaneology* includes 25 fabulous ways to get you started. Whether you're a sewing whiz or an amateur whose last project involved popsicle sticks and finger paint, the projects in *Jeaneology* will have you falling in love with your old blues all over again.

TOOLBOX and TERMS

NECESSITIES FOR ALL PROJECTS

These are items you will need for nearly every project in this book. It is a good idea to have them on hand in a little kit or container. (Try making a zippered pouch like the one on page 64 to carry them in!)

Chalk pencil: You need this to mark off measurements with your ruler. Go for a pale color, which is more likely to show up on dark fabrics.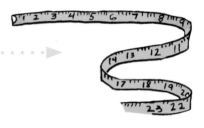

Flexible measuring tape: The best kind of measuring tapes for sewing look like long, sturdy, flexible ribbons marked with inches and centimeters. Typically, they are yellow, though they come in a variety of colors. They are inexpensive and easy to find, and indispensable for measuring around curves.

Iron: Any household iron will do. You can either use an ironing board or put a towel over a hard surface like the floor or a table.

Pins: These are key for holding things in place before you sew them. Long pins with little balls on top work well. When you sew your pinned-together layers in place, remember to take the pins out as you secure the layers together with stitching!

Ruler: This is needed for measuring lengths and widths, and customizing the projects to fit you and your stuff.

Sewing machine and/or heavy-duty sewing needle: Because jeans are so sturdy, sewing them by hand can be a chore. Some of the smaller projects in this book are a breeze for hand-sewing, but everything will go faster if you can get behind a sewing machine. Either way, be sure to use a heavy-duty needle.

Sharp scissors: Jeans are thick and sturdy, so sharp shears are a must.

Thread: Some projects call for thread to match your jeans, others for contrasting colors (hues that will stand out), and some for both. These are just guidelines. Get creative and experiment with different thread colors whenever you think a project calls for it.

SPECIAL TOOLS AND MATERIALS

These are things you'll need for only some of the projects in the book.

Batting: This is a thick, squishy fabric made of either cotton or cotton-polyester fibers that quilters use as an inner layer to make their quilts puffy and warm. Batting is specifically meant to be sewn between fabrics so that you don't see it; therefore, it isn't pretty to look at. You can buy it by the yard or in a large package at a fabric or quilt shop. Use any type of batting for the projects in this book.

Bias tape: Though it is called tape, bias tape is not sticky. Packaged bias tape is fabric that has been cut, folded, and ironed specifically to be used for finishing off the raw edges of seams, or binding multiple sewn layers of fabric.

Decorative extras: Some projects are only really finished when you've added your own personal touch. So when you are at the thrift, fabric, or craft store, keep an eye out for buttons, pins, patches, ribbons, sequins, and any other add-ons that reflect your style. By attaching these extras, you will make your projects truly individual.

Seam ripper: This is a nifty little gadget that makes pulling out seams much easier. You can find one at a fabric or craft store. It is basically a handle with a hook on one end that rips out the stitches of the seams you wish to pull apart. Seam rippers typically come with instructions included.

Zippers and zipper tape: You can buy zippers of different colors and lengths at most fabric stores. The zipper consists of two sets of teeth that hook together when you pull the zipper closed. Each set of teeth is attached to a fabric strip that you stitch to the project you are working on. This fabric strip is called the **zipper tape.**

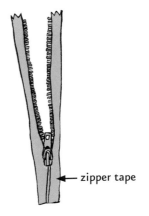

← zipper tape

SEWING TERMS

Below is some sewing vocabulary you'll want to know before you get started on the projects.

Alternate fabric: This means any fabric being used in a project that is *not* blue jeans.

Contrasting fabric: This term refers to a bright or patterned fabric that looks very different from your blue jeans fabric.

Contrasting thread: This is thread in a color that will stand out against your blue jeans.

Clip corners: This expression means to cut off the pointy triangle of a newly sewn corner. The cut will end up being on the *inside* of one of your projects.

The reason you do it: When you sew a point or an angle on the inside of your project (a corner of a pillow, for instance), you want that corner to be pointy and smooth when you turn the project **right side out**. Therefore, you'll need to clip away the **seam allowance** *before turning* the fabric right side out, so that the inside of the corner can not bunch up. To do this, simply take your scissors and cut off the little triangle that forms the point of the corner. (The book will instruct you when this is necessary.) Just be careful not to cut across the stitches themselves.

Edges (long and short): Many of these projects include roughly rectangular-shaped pieces of fabric. As we learned in grade school, rectangles have two long sides and two short sides. In sewing terms, we call those sides long edge(s) and short edge(s).

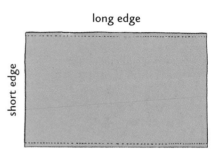

long edge

short edge

Hem: The hem is the name for the seam sewn at the bottom of pant legs, skirts, and shirts. *Hem* can also be used as a verb when you're talking about changing this seam to make pants or a skirt longer or shorter — for example, when you shorten your jeans, you hem them.

Pattern: People who sew often buy paper patterns to help them cut out pieces of fabric the right size and shape for what they are making. You can find these at most fabric or craft stores. You won't need to buy any paper patterns for the projects in this book, but you will be making patterns of your own by tracing shapes onto paper, and sometimes right onto your jeans fabric. Sometimes these are referred to as pattern pieces.

Raw edge: This is a cut edge of the fabric and will fray if left unsewn. Cutoff shorts have raw edges.

Right and wrong sides: "Right side" indicates the good side of the fabric — for example, the denim that shows on the outside of your jeans. "Wrong side" is like the inside of the fabric, or the part of the fabric that is washed out or without the design. For some fabrics, either side will do. But for many, there is a right and a wrong side. This book will frequently direct you to place pieces **right sides together** or **wrong sides together**.

Note: *When the instruction has to do with right and left, it will say "right-hand side."*

Right sides together/wrong sides together: Sometimes you will be instructed to pin pieces of fabric "right sides together," which means that you will place one piece of fabric right (or good) side up, and the other on top of it good side down and then pin. "Wrong sides together" indicates just the opposite, one piece wrong side up, the other on top of it wrong side down.

Seam: This is a line of stitching that joins and holds two, three, or more layers of fabric together. When we talk about the "inseam" of a pair of jeans, we're referring to the single continuous seam that holds the jeans together under the zipper and along the inside of the legs. The seams that run down the outside of your legs are the outer seams.

Seam allowance: This is the distance between the raw edges of fabrics you are sewing together and the **seam**.

Turning: Sometimes turning just means flipping something from side to side or turning something inside out. But there is another meaning for *turning* that's specific to sewing. When we don't want the seams to show after we've sewn two pieces together, we first sew them inside out and then turn them right side out. In these cases, we leave a hole in the seam for turning, and we pull the whole project through that hole to turn it right side out.

Leave a hole in the seam, like this.

Time and Difficulty Icons

Below are the icons included in each project to symbolize the approximate time each project takes and the level of complexity.

= quick project

= not so quick project

= lengthy project

= easy project

= not so easy project

= difficult project

ROCKIN' RAGS

TAKING OLD BLUE JEANS
FROM TEAR TO WEAR

Jeans are the queen of the closet. They rule over your other clothes. When you are getting dressed, you decide what length shirt to wear depending on how high (or low) your jeans rise, and the length of your pant legs determines whether you wear flats or heels. Jeans are very important to a girl's wardrobe. And, now, the queen of the closet is about to expand her rule.

In this chapter, you'll learn how to glam up jeans that make you yawn, refashion jeans that scream preppie perfect, and hippify an old pair of peg legs into peace and love flares. You'll also learn how to transform a pair of jeans into a long, bohemian skirt (nice when they get too snug in the legs) or turn them into a flapper-style fringed short skirt (great for those jeans that feel a bit short). While the main idea is to recycle what you already have in your wardrobe, you may eventually find yourself heading to the thrift store to buy new (old) jeans — just to cut them up and remake them into a custom-fit, designed-by-you fashion masterpiece.

BOHEMIAN CHIC SKIRT

What could be freer and flirtier than a long, pretty skirt made from old blue jeans and some fun, feminine fabric? This is an ideal project for that pair of jeans you called your favorite ... until they started hugging your hips just a little too much. With a simple yard of fabric, you can now transform those old jeans into a comfy, flowy skirt.

WHAT YOU'LL NEED:

* 1 pair of jeans
* 1 yard contrasting fun fabric (Choose a fabric that is not too slippery or stretchy, since that can be difficult to sew. A mid-weight cotton or polyester should work well.)
* seam ripper

TIME

DIFFICULTY

PART 1: FROM PANTS TO SKIRT

In order to begin making your skirt, you'll need to cut out the inseam of the jeans, so that they are held together along only the outer side seams.

1 Starting at the bottom of one leg and keeping close to the inner seams of the jean legs cut all the way up one leg, across the center seam, and down the other leg. When you are finished, the legs will be held together only by the outer seams.

cut here ↗

2 Since the double-stitched inner seam is so thick, you'll want to cut it out altogether. Use your scissors to cut out this inner seam, starting from one side and ending at the other.

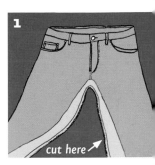

cut seam out, like this

You'll notice now that the remaining center seam below the zipper curls under. In order to turn the jeans into a skirt, you must flatten this seam. You will do this in steps 3–6.

3 Using a seam ripper, take out the double stitching of the remaining center seam below the zipper a few stitches at a time. Every few stitches, test to see if the top fabric of the seam will lie flat. It will curve over to the left as it flattens out and overlap the opposite leg.

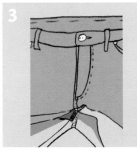

4 Once you get it to lie flat, pin it in this position.

5 Stitch it into place along both lines left by the stitching you ripped out.

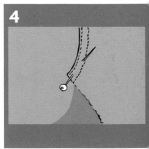

6 Repeat this process to flatten and secure the center seam of the rear of the jeans.

7 Turn your jeans inside out. Fold the raw edges of the front inner jean legs to the inside by ½" and iron them flat.

PART 2: CUTTING THE CLOTH

At this point there is a triangular gap between the jean legs. You will measure this gap in order to determine what size piece of contrasting fabric is needed to fill it in the front and the back.

8 Turn jeans right side out and flatten them on your work surface. Measure the distance from the center seam under the zipper to the hem and add 3".

9 At the bottom of the jeans, measure the gap between the raw edge of the left front jean leg and the raw edge of the right-hand front jean leg and add 2".

10 Cut two pieces of your contrasting fabric that each measure the length of the measurement you reached in step 8 and the width of the measurement you reached in step 9. One piece will be for the front, the other for the back.

PART 3: FILLING THE GAP

Here you'll use the pieces of contrasting fabric you just cut to fill the triangular gaps in the jeans front and back.

11 Slide this length of contrasting fabric between the front and back of the jeans, centering it to fill the triangular gap between the two inner edges of the jean leg fronts.

12 Pin the fabric in place under the jean front along the folded edge of the ironed-under leg edges, being careful not to pin together the front and back of the jeans.

13 Sew fabric into place, stitching close to the fold of the jeans edge.

14 Repeat to fill the space in the rear of the jeans.

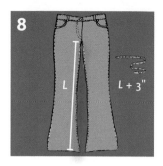

STEP 8 × STEP 9 =
SIZE OF
CONTRASTING
FABRIC

PART 4: FRAYED OR FINISHED?

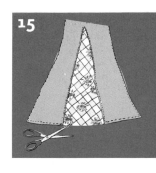

At this point you can either trim the excess contrasting fabric at the bottom of the skirt for a frayed look or hem it for a more finished look.

15 For a frayed look, simply trim away the excess contrasting fabric at the bottom of the skirt so that it is even with the hem of the jean fabric. · · · · · · · · · · · · · · · · · · ▷

16 For a finished look, hem the skirt by folding the frayed contrasting fabric that's hanging down at the bottom inside the skirt until the fold is in line with the jeans hem. Then, stitch into place using a ½" seam allowance. After you've hemmed it, trim away excess fabric around the seams inside the skirt. · ▷

17 Put on your comfortable new skirt and head out for a sunny afternoon lounging in the park!

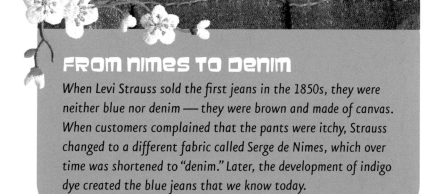

FROM NIMES TO DENIM

When Levi Strauss sold the first jeans in the 1850s, they were neither blue nor denim — they were brown and made of canvas. When customers complained that the pants were itchy, Strauss changed to a different fabric called Serge de Nimes, which over time was shortened to "denim." Later, the development of indigo dye created the blue jeans that we know today.

SHORT and Sassy SKIRT

It is definitely a sad day when your formerly favorite jeans get an unwelcome hole in the knee or shrink up past your ankle. But don't despair—they can still be saved. Instead of retiring them, give them new life as a super sassy skirt with a fun flapper fringe.

WHAT YOU'LL NEED:

* 1 pair of jeans
* 2 yards of fringe

TIME

DIFFICULTY

Part 1: How Short Do You Want It?

Here you will determine how short you'd like your skirt to be, then cut the jean legs off evenly so you can get started.

1 Put on your jeans and measure from the top of the waistband down to where you'd like the skirt to fall on your legs. Add 1".

2 Remove your jeans. Take the total measurement and, using your ruler and chalk, mark this distance on the front of one jean leg, starting from the waistband at both the inner and outer seams. Connect these marks into a line. Repeat on the other jean leg.

3 Cut through both layers of the jean legs along the line you drew and set aside the remaining material for later. • • • • • • • •

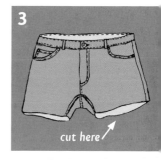

cut here

Part 2: From Shorts to Skirt

In order to begin making your skirt, you'll need to cut out the inseam of the jeans, so that the jeans are held together along only the outer side seams.

cut here

4 Starting at the raw edge of one leg and keeping close to the inner seams of the jean legs, cut all the way up one leg, across the center seam and down the other leg. When you are finished, the legs will be held together only by the outer seams. •

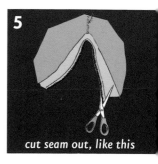

cut seam out, like this

5 Since the double-stitched inner seam is so thick, you'll want to cut it out altogether. Use your scissors to cut out this inner seam, starting from one side and ending at the other. •

You'll notice now that the remaining center seam below the zipper curls under. In order to turn the jeans into a skirt, you must flatten this seam. You will do this in steps 6–9.

6 Using a seam ripper, take out the double stitching of the remaining center seam below the zipper a few stitches at a time. Every few stitches, test to see if the top fabric of the seam will lie flat. It will curve over to the left as it flattens out and overlap the opposite leg. • • • • • • • • • • • • • • • •

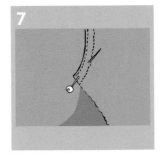

7 Once you get it to lie flat, pin it in this position. • • • • • • • •

8 Stitch it into place along both lines left by the stitching you ripped out.

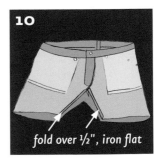

9 Repeat this process to flatten and secure the center seam of the rear of the jeans.

10 Turn your jeans inside out. Fold the raw edges of the front inner jean legs to the inside ½" and iron them flat. • • • • •

PART 3: FILLING THE GAP

Now you will use the jean legs that you cut off to fill the triangular openings in the jean front and back.

11 Grab one jean leg. Cut the seams and hem off one layer of your jean leg to get one single-layered, rectangular piece of seamless jean. •

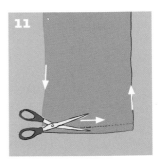

fold over ½", iron flat

12 Turn your jeans right side out again, and slide this rectangle between the front and back of the jeans so that it fills the triangular open space between the turned-under raw edges of the front jean legs. It may hang down below the bottom seam, which is fine. •▶

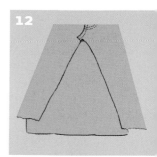

13 When you are satisfied with how it fills the space, pin it in place. Be careful not to catch the back of the jeans in your pins, as you don't want to sew the front and back together! • • • • • • • •▶

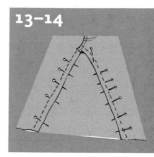

14 Stitch together the front of the jeans and the inserted rectangle of denim close to the folded edge of the jeans. Start at the raw hem of one leg, going up and across the center seam, and down to the other raw edge.

15 Trim the bottom of the rectangle so that it is even with the raw edges on either side. •

16 Repeat steps 10–15 to fill the triangular gap in the back. • • •▶

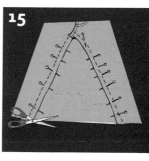

PART 4: ADDING THE SHIMMY

Instead of hemming the skirt, you'll attach flapper-style fringe to the bottom. The hem of the skirt will fray, but this will mix in with the fringe to give it a worn, funky look.

17 Using your ruler and chalk, make a line 1" above the raw hem, around the entire bottom of the skirt.

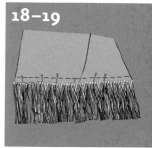

18 Pin the top, sewn-together edge of the fringe along this line. •▶

19 Sew the fringe to the jean hem, stitching close to the lines of thread along the top of the fringe.

20 Try your skirt on. Shimmy to see the fringe do its thing!

OH, DaISY! SHORTS

Even if you're too young to remember the TV version of *The Dukes of Hazzard*, you've probably heard of Daisy Duke: that fictional Southern sister with platform sandals and great legs who made jean shorts famous. Here's your chance to play like Daisy. Made from an old pair of jeans, these shorts can be crafted in the simple cut-and-frayed style or updated with an attention-grabbing, colorful ribbon hem.

WHAT YOU'LL NEED:

* ✷ 1 pair of jeans
* ✷ ribbon (enough to wrap around the widest part of your thigh twice with a little bit left over)

TIME

DIFFICULTY

PART 1: SHOW A LITTLE LEG — OR A LOT

Here you'll determine how short you'd like your shorts, then cut off the jean legs accordingly.

1 Put on your jeans and measure from the top of the waistband down to where you'd like the shorts to fall on your legs. (It's better to err on the side of longer; it's way easier to trim them down if they are too long than to add length if you cut them too short.) After you have your measurement, add 1".

2 Remove your jeans. Take the total measurement and, using your ruler and chalk, mark the front of one jean leg this distance from the waistband at both the inner and outer seams. Connect these marks into a line. Repeat on the other jean leg.

3 Cut through both layers of both jean legs along the lines you drew. • ▶

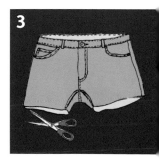

4 Try the jeans on to make sure they fall just where you want them to. Trim them if they are too long. You can leave the shorts as is, or you can dress them up by adding on the ribbon hem (see below).

PART 2: ADD A LITTLE FLAIR

Here you'll attach a length of ribbon to the raw edges at the bottom of your shorts.

5 Starting at the inside seam of one shorts leg, place the ribbon on the jeans by matching the bottom edge of the ribbon with the raw edge of the shorts leg. Pin the ribbon around the circumference of the leg. • • • • • • • • • • • • • ▶

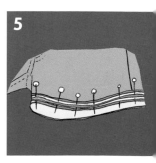

6 To hide the raw end of the ribbon, fold it to the inside and pin it so it butts up against the ribbon where you began. • • •▶

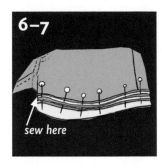

6–7

sew here

7 Using thread that matches the ribbon, sew the ribbon to the shorts leg, stitching as close to the top of the ribbon as possible.

8 Turn the shorts inside out and fold the raw jean edge up so it exposes the ribbon completely. Pin into place. • • • • • • •

9 Using thread that matches the jeans, sew this folded hem to the shorts leg, stitching about ¼" away from the fold. Repeat steps 5–9 on other leg.

8–9

sew here

10 Voilà! Check out your new, frayless jean shorts with their kick-butt ribbon hem, and don't be surprised if people start calling you Daisy.

DON'T CUT UP GRANDPA'S JEANS!

Since jeans have become such a fashion icon, the value of antique jeans to collectors has gone sky-high. Good-condition 19th-century jeans have sold at antique auctions for as much as $100,000. So, if a relative offers you a pair of jeans that belonged to your great-great grandmother or grandfather, do some research before you use them for scrap!

FUNKY FLARES

If you have been staring lately into a closet filled with tapered-leg jeans and yearning for something with a little more flare, yearn no longer. With some fun fabric, a seam ripper, and a few stitches, you can have a handmade pair of flares in no time.

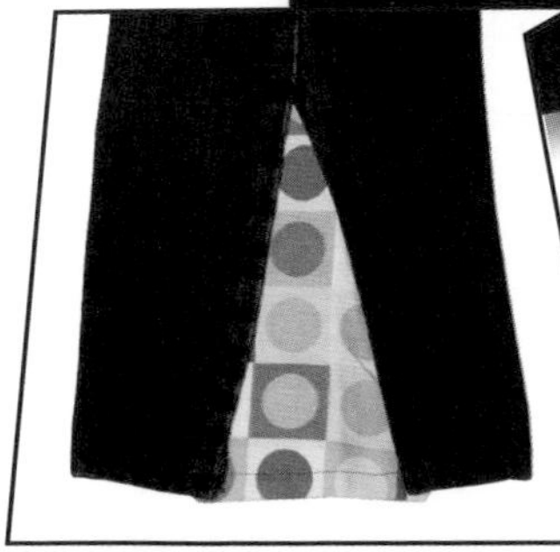

TIME

DIFFICULTY

WHAT YOU'LL NEED:

* 1 pair of straight-leg or tapered-leg jeans

* ½-yard of contrasting funky fabric
  (A fun-print cotton would work well, as would patterned velour or heavy polyester satin. If you want these jeans to be machine washable, be sure to wash and dry this fabric before starting the project.)

* seam ripper

Part 1: Flaring Out

In order to make the jeans flare at the bottom, you need to open up the outside seam of each leg so you can insert extra fabric.

1 Using a seam ripper, rip open the outside seam of one jean leg to about 4"–8" from the bottom, depending on where you want the flare to start on your leg. · · · · · · · · · · · · · · · · · ▶

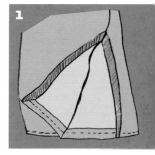

2 Fold under the raw edges of this seam ½" and pin in place.

Part 2: Brightening Your Bell

Once you've created a flared opening in the jean leg, you'll use your funky fabric to fill it and make the bottom of the jean leg bell out.

3 Cut out a rectangle of the fabric that measures 6"×10".

4 Slide the rectangle of fabric inside one jean leg. · · · · · · · · · · · ▶

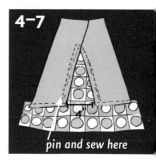

pin and sew here

5 Adjust so that the edges of the jean hem are 4" apart and the fabric fills the triangular space made by the separated side seams. Some fabric should extend beyond the jean hem and above the top of the triangle.

6 Pin the folded jean edges to the fabric, being careful not to catch the other side of the jean leg in your pins. You don't want to sew the leg shut!

7 Sew the jean leg to the fabric, stitching close to the folded edge of the jeans.

8 Fold the remaining length of fabric (which falls below the jean hem) inside the jean leg until the fold is even with the jean hem.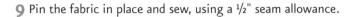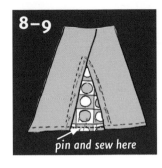

9 Pin the fabric in place and sew, using a ½" seam allowance.

10 Turn the bottom of the jean leg inside out and trim any excess fabric away from the two side seams (where the flare was attached) and the hem.

11 Repeat all steps on your second jean leg.

12 Put on your new old funky flares and a rockin' pair of platforms, and head out for a night on the dance floor.

TELL IT TO THE MARINES: THE ORIGINS OF BELL BOTTOMS

Jean lovers have sailors to thank for bell bottoms and flares. Originally, U.S. Navy sailors wore flared pants because the wider bottom made wet pants easier to take off over shoes and boots. This meant that if you fell overboard, you could have your pants off in a hurry for easier swimming. In the 1960s, hippies started buying clothes from Army-Navy surplus stores. They liked the style of these naval castoffs so much that they even began sewing triangular patches into their regular jeans to make them bell out.

Keep Your Blue Jeans Blue

Sometimes you want your jeans to look washed out, but not always. What about those crisp dark-wash jeans that you actually don't want to fade with every wash? Here are some jean-washing tricks to keep your blue jeans blue.

* Before washing, snap, zip, or button the jeans closed, which will keep the zipper or other closures from snagging or rubbing the fabric and making pale spots.

* Turn them inside out to protect the good side from rubbing up against other fabrics and losing color.

* Wash them in cold water with a cold rinse. This allows less color to wash away. Use the gentle cycle so that they aren't agitated any more than necessary.

* Hang them to dry. If they get stiff after air-drying, throw them in the dryer under a no-heat setting for five minutes or so to soften them up.

eMBeLLISH IT!

So you want new jeans. But when you consult your pocketbook, it tells you it's a no-go. Don't panic. With a little bit of creativity and some inexpensive trim, you can bring new, glamorous life to your old jeans in no time.

WHAT YOU'LL NEED:

* 1 pair of jeans
* 4 yards ribbon trim
  (sequin, sparkly, or any other eye-catching trim found at the local craft or fabric store)

TIME 🕐🕐🕐

DIFFICULTY

Part 1: Get in Line

In this first step, you will cover the seams running down the outside of your pant leg with your hand-selected trim, then sew the trim in place.

1 Position and pin the length of the trim so that it covers and hides the outer seam of one jean leg. Repeat for the second jean leg. • ►

2 Hand stitch the trim to your jean leg using small stitches along the edges of the trim. Be careful not to catch the opposite side of the leg in your stitches or you can sew the leg shut.

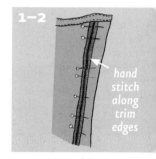

1-2

hand stitch along trim edges

Part 2: Top It Off

Now you'll glam up the top of the jeans by adding trim just below the waistband.

3 Pin the trim under the waistband around the entire circumference of your jeans. • ►

4 To hide the raw end of the trim, fold it behind the flap that covers the zipper.

5 Sew the ribbon into place, starting from the flap that covers the zipper and going around the entire circumference. Sew only along the top edge of your trim so that you can get into your pockets if you need to!

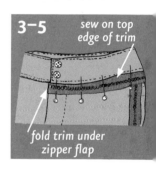

3-5

sew on top edge of trim

fold trim under zipper flap

6 When you have sewn all around the waistband and reached the zipper again, make sure that the raw end of the trim is hidden under the zipper flap and that it matches up with the beginning of the trim when the zipper is closed. Sew the end of the trim in place. • • • • • • • • • • • • • • • • • • •

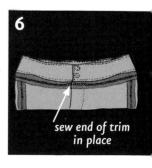

6

sew end of trim in place

7 Put on your jazzy jeans and head out to party! And remember: Sparkly or sequined trim should not be put in the washing machine, so be sure to hand wash these jeans from now on.

Get Distressed

Have you ever noticed that sometimes jeans with holes, spots, and stains actually cost more than those in mint condition? It seems designers have caught on to the fact that we love our jeans best when they are worn in — and that we'll pay extra not to have to wait 100 washes to wear them in ourselves. Designers call the process of prematurely aging jeans "distressing" them. Of course, the real distressing part is how much we shell out to buy them. So why not distress yourself? To turn a pair of crisp blues into second-hand look-alikes, all you need is a disposable razor, some bleach, the following four tricks, and a vision of true antiquity.

WHAT YOU'LL NEED:

* 1 pair of jeans
* disposable razor
* bleach with Q-tip or bleach pen
* stencil

TIME

DIFFICULTY

PART 1: FAIR WEATHERING

Weathering is a science — even when it comes to jeans. The most flattering way to weather your jeans is to create a lighter patch down the front of each thigh. This pale space, framed by the darker denim on your inner and outer thighs, will create an illusion that makes your thighs look slimmer. And all without a diet!

The fastest way to get this look is with a disposable razor. (Just make sure that you throw the razor away when you are done, as it will be very dull and quite painful if used to shave any human parts.)

1 With the jeans off, use the razor in the same motion as if you were actually shaving your leg — though you're shaving off bits of jean instead. Focus on the space about 2" in from the inner and outer thigh seams, shaving in gentle strokes and blowing the jean fuzz away from the razor as you go.

2 Stop shaving when the area is about one shade lighter than the dark inner and outer seams, or when it begins to wear small holes through the fabric, whichever comes first. Don't be disappointed if your jeans don't look much different; you will really notice the change after you wash and dry the jeans.

3 Use the razor in the same way to distress the tops of pockets and the bottom hem.

PART 2: WANT HOLES?

It's something your mother will never understand, but holey knees are bound to please. Here's how to do it.

1 Put the jeans on, bend your knees, and mark the area where your kneecaps hit the denim.

2 Take the jeans off, place a book or other impervious object in the jean leg under the marks, and use the razor on this area in a back and forth motion until holes begin to form.

3 When the holes are big enough, use your fingers to gently rip apart any fabric that remains between them and create a hole from seam to seam. If the fabric is still too tough to rip, you can help this process along with scissors. After a few washes, your holey knees will look like you really earned them.

Part 3: Whisked Away

Designer jeans are often "whiskered," a fancy term for the pale streaks designers put in the places jeans would naturally crease and whiten over time. This is an extremely easy effect to create using a bleach pen, or bleach and a cotton swab.

Safety note: Bleach is very toxic. It is also corrosive and stains badly. Be sure to wear rubber gloves, cover your work surface in newspaper, and wear your oldest clothes so you won't be sad if the bleach gets on you. If you are using a bleach pen, the bleach will be in a gel formula and will stay where you put it on the surface of the fabric. With liquid bleach and a cotton swab method, you may want to stuff your jeans with newspaper to prevent your designs from bleeding to the back if you don't want them there.

1 Put your jeans on and stand, lifting one leg up so that your thigh is parallel to the ground. Draw a chalk pencil line through the creases created by this movement.

2 Repeat with the opposite leg.

3 Sit down in the jeans and draw chalk pencil lines through any new creases created by this position.

4 Remove your jeans and lay them on a work surface covered with newsprint.

5 Using a bleach pen or the bleach-saturated cotton swab, draw bleach over the pencil lines, extending them from the side seam to the center seam, taking care to make them look natural and uneven as real wrinkles are. • • • • • • • • • • • • • • • • • • ▶

6 Allow the jeans to sit with bleach marks on them for 5–10 minutes, then wash them alone in the washing machine. Your results: Designer jean whiskers at a bargain-basement price.

PART 4: STYLISH STENCILING

Want to get more creative with your bleach pen? Grab a stencil and turn your jeans into an abstract work of art — or, if you like to doodle, go freehand and see where your imagination takes you. This works best on darker jeans so that the bleached designs really pop.

1 Lay your stencil on the jeans and blot the open areas with the bleach pen or the bleach-soaked cotton swab until you have filled the design. • ▶

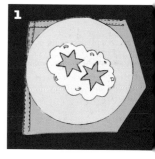

2 Keep moving and blotting the stencil around your jeans until you are satisfied with the patterns and shapes that arise.

3 Add a freestyle bleach drawing, if you like.

4 Allow the jeans to sit undisturbed for at least 5 minutes. (More time means whiter, more developed bleach designs, so if you want them to show up very strongly, wait at least 10 minutes.)

5 Put your jeans in the washing machine alone, as they will bleach or bleed color onto anything you put in with them.

6 Remove them from the washer and dry to see the fruits of your labor.

Tie One On Necktie

Usually, a necktie brings to mind a buttoned-up business man in a three-piece suit. But businessmen aren't the only ones who get to wear ties. In fact, they're often worn by cool chicks as a rebellious fashion statement. What better way to dress down this ultimate accessory in workday attire than to make one out of a pair of jeans? Don't worry if you don't know how to tie the perfect knot — this project can also work as a belt and a hair tie.

WHAT YOU'LL NEED:

* 1 pair of jeans

* 1 necktie
  (can be found for a dollar or so at most thrift stores)

* decorative extras

TIME 🕐🕐

DIFFICULTY

PART 1: CUTTING THE CLOTH

It is unlikely you'll find a pair of jeans with legs long enough to make the entire tie, so you'll make your tie in stages. You'll use a ready-made tie as a pattern to make the pieces.

1 Before you get started, cut off the bottom hem of the jeans.

2 Starting at the top of the jeans, just below the pocket, pin the tie to the front of one jean leg, going straight down the center. The widest part of the tie should be attached at the top. • ▶

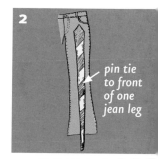

pin tie to front of one jean leg

3 Continue pinning the tie to the jean leg until you reach the raw edge of the jean where the hem used to be. You will have a lot of tie hanging over, but leave it there for the time being.

4 Trace around the portion of the tie that you have pinned to the jean leg.

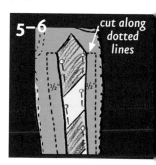

cut along dotted lines

5-6

½" ½"

5 Measure and make marks ½" away from the side of the tie all along the sides. (Don't make marks around the wide point of the tie that is attached at the top of the jean leg, only along the sides.) Join these marks into a second outline ½" away from original tie tracing. • • • • • • • • • • • • • • • • •

6 Cut along this second, outer outline, and also along the actual wide pointed end of the tie to create your first half of the jean tie.

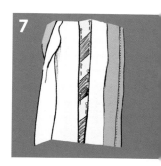

7 Pin the remaining part of the tie to the second layer of jean leg. • ▶

8 Repeat steps 4, 5, and 6 with the back portion of the tie to create your second half of the jean tie.

PART 2: PUTTING IT TOGETHER

You'll sew together the pieces you cut out to make the length of the tie, then hem the two long sides of the tie so that they don't fray. The pointy ends of the tie will be left to fray for a rugged, dressed-down effect.

9 Unpin the original tie from the two lengths of the new denim tie.

10 Pin together the two lengths to make one long tie. Pin at the narrowest ends (the straight ends), leaving a ½" seam allowance, with the right sides facing each other.

11 Sew the pieces together at the ends leaving the ½" seam allowance with which you pinned them. • • • • • • • • • • • • •▶

12 Unfold the two lengths of the tie with the wrong side facing you. Open the seam and iron flat.

13 Turn the jean tie right side up, and fold the long, raw edges under along your original tracing line. Pin into place.

14 To hem, stitch down the raw edges, sewing close to the fold. •▶

15 Embellish your tie with ribbon, lace, or a painted design. Match it with a cute denim skirt and give new meaning to business casual!

TIES THROUGH THE AGES

While they have changed in length and width over the years, neckties, as we know them today, first came into men's fashion in the 1920s. If you don't know how to tie a necktie, it is very easy to learn. If you can't find a male in your household to show you, there are photographic tutorials on the Internet — just type "how to tie a necktie" into your favorite search engine to find one.

mean Jean accessories

LETTING YOUR ACCESSORIES
SING THE BLUES

Every girl has a stack of defunct jeans in her closet, the members of which are either torn beyond recognition, unforgivably out of style, or simply don't fit anymore. You probably have the stack, too — and you just can't bring yourself to throw it away. Well, now you don't have to. Those very same dead threads can be magically transformed into a hair band, a handbag, a bracelet, or a cell phone case. Everything that makes jeans great — multiple pockets, sturdy construction, and that goes-with-everything style — makes them great for accessories, too.

HeaDSTRONG HaIR BanD

Is your hair between trims? Limp and lifeless? Fluffy and frizzy? If you're feeling like your mane is a little under the weather, you'll be happy to know that the doctor is in the house — and she's prescribing this hair band. It is the perfect remedy to liven up your locks. It's quick to whip up and guaranteed to cure any hair problem — at least for a little while.

WHAT YOU'LL NEED:

* 1 jean leg
* 4" piece of elastic
* decorative extras

TIME 🕐

DIFFICULTY

Part 1: Cutting and Trimming

Using the given measurements, you'll cut and shape the two rectangular pieces of denim that will make up your hair band.

1 Cut two one-layer strips of denim from the jean leg; each should measure about 16" long and 3" wide. • • • • • • • • • • • • • • • • • • •▶

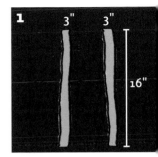

2 Make them each a slightly oval shape by tapering them from 3" wide in the center to 2" wide at each end. • • • • • • • • • • • •

Part 2: Making a Tube

Now you'll sew the pieces together to create a tube that is open on both ends.

3 Pin the strips with the right sides together and make a tube by sewing together along both long edges.

4 Turn right side out and iron flat.

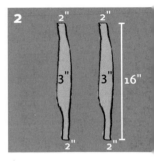

Part 3: Attaching the Elastic

Here you'll attach the elastic at the open ends of the tube and sew across to secure.

5 Turn about ½" of raw edges of one short edge into the tube.

6 Insert elastic in middle of the opening, also about ½". Close the tube, and pin the ends in place. • • • • • • • • • • • • • • • • •▶

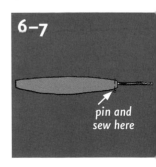

pin and sew here

7 Sew across, close to the edge, to close the opening.

8 Repeat on the other side.

9 Give it your own signature style by sewing on sequins, gluing on ribbon or rickrack, painting it, or stenciling it with a bleach pen.

GIRL ON THE GO MP3 PLAYER AND CELL PHONE POCKET

When a girl is on the move, ease is of the essence. You have to be able to just throw your stuff in a bag and head out. Of course, mobile phones and MP3 players don't take kindly to being tossed. This accessory will keep your electronic necessities safe in your bag—and dressed in a designer blues style all its very own.

WHAT YOU'LL NEED:

* 1 jean leg
* 1 piece of felt
* 1 button
* 1 elastic ponytail holder
* pinking shears
* decorative extras
* The size of your gadget will determine the size of the pocket.

TIME

DIFFICULTY

Part 1: Cutting the Cloth

You'll cut out the basic pieces for your pouch.

1 Grab your jean leg. Cut the seams and the hem off of one layer of your jean leg to get one single-layered, rectangular piece of seamless jean. Cut it to measure 13" long. • • • • • • • • • • •▶

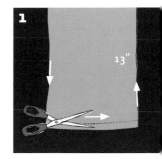

2 Using this one-layer rectangle as a pattern, cut a piece of felt the same size.

3 Lay the denim rectangle on your work surface wrong side up, and lay the felt down on top of it.

Part 2: Designing Your Pocket

You'll use your gadget as a guide to help you measure and mark off the perimeters of the pocket and flap.

4 Place your gadget in the center of the rectangle and pull the two layers of fabric up from the bottom to make a pocket that reaches the top of the gadget. The remaining fabric above will be the flap. •▶

5 To define the top of the pocket, make a chalk line where the raw edge of jeans (pulled over the gadget) comes into contact with the felt (above the gadget). Remove the gadget, leaving the fabric folded up to the line you just marked.

6 To create sewing lines for the sides of the pocket, lay the gadget on top of the fabric pocket and make marks ½" away from the sides of the gadget. Connect the marks you just made to make two parallel chalk lines running up each side of the pocket. •▶

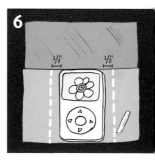

47

PART 3: SEWING THE POCKET

First you'll sew together the two layers of denim and felt at the bottom, then you'll fold this seam up to the top pocket line and sew the four layers of denim and felt together along the sides.

7 Unfold denim and felt rectangle. At bottom edge, stitch between the chalk lines, leaving a ¼" seam allowance from the raw edges.

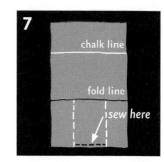

8 Bring this newly sewn edge back up to the pocket line you drew earlier in step 5. Pin together the pocket along parallel chalk lines, then sew, stitching along the lines. Now you should have your pocket.

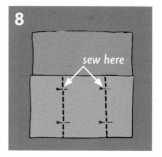

PART 4: MAKING THE FLAP

You'll mark sewing lines for the flap, insert the elastic closure, and sew the closure in place by stitching across the top of the flap.

9 With the flap open, draw lines on the felt that extend upward from the already stitched side lines of the bottom pocket. Extend these lines to the top of the flap.

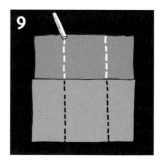

10 Tie a knot in the middle of the elastic hair band, and pin half of it between the felt and jean layers at the top of the flap, centered between the chalk lines.

11 Pin the flap layers together and sew along one chalk line, then across the top, using a ½" seam allowance, and down the other chalk line.

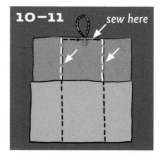

PART 5: FINISHING TOUCHES

Since the edges of the pocket extend beyond the sides of the gadget, you'll trim away the excess fabric with pinking shears to minimize fraying. Then you'll find the right spot for the button closure.

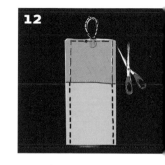

12 Using pinking shears, cut away excess fabric around the sides of the pocket you've sewn and along the top of the flap, making sure not to cut your hair band buttonhole. • • • • • • • • • ▶

13 Put your gadget in the pocket, and lower the flap. Mark where the center of the elastic loop hits the front of the pocket and sew your button on there.

14 Add patches, fabric paint, or decorative buttons, then pop in your phone or MP3 player and bop on out the door.

PLENTIFUL POCKETS HANDBAG

Need more pockets? This hip handbag will do the trick. Made out of the most pocketful part of a pair of jeans, this bag will help you keep all of your stuff organized and at your fingertips.

WHAT YOU'LL NEED:

* 1 pair of jeans
* ½-yard of contrasting fabric for lining (either fabric from the store or old sheets will work fine)
* seam ripper
* decorative extras

TIME 🕐🕐🕐

DIFFICULTY

Part 1: Constructing the Body of the Bag

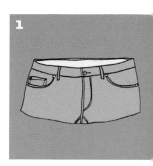

You'll cut off the jean legs evenly, like supershort shorts, then sew the bottom together to create the body of the bag.

1 Mark a line on the jean legs about 1" below where the center seam hits. Cut the legs off at the line. (Put jean legs aside—you will need one of them to make the straps later on.)

2 Take the supershort shorts and cut across the center seam in a straight line so that there is no longer a separation between the legs.

You'll notice now that the remaining center seam below the zipper curls under. In order to make the jeans into a bag, you must flatten out this seam. You will do this in steps 3–6.

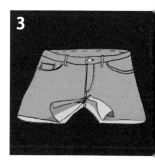

3 Using a seam ripper, take out the double stitching of the remaining center seam below the zipper a few stitches at a time. Every few stitches, test to see if the seam will lie flat. It will curve over to the left as it flattens out and overlap the opposite leg.

4 Once you get it to lie flat, pin it in this position.

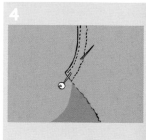

5 Stitch it into place along both lines left by the stitching you ripped out.

6 Repeat this process to flatten and secure the center seam of the rear of the jeans.

7 Turn the jeans inside out and sew the front and back together in a straight line across the raw bottom edge. (You may need to trim the remaining fabric from the cut-off

legs along the bottom to make an even line from side seam to side seam across the center seam.)

8 Turn right side out.

Part 2: Lining Your Bag

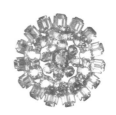

Using the bag body you just made as a pattern, you'll create a lining from your contrasting fabric. You will then sew the lining into the bag body.

9 Fold your contrasting fabric in half, wrong sides together, and lay the bag body you just made on top of it.

10 On the contrasting fabric, make marks ½" away from the bag body, all the way around it. Remove the bag body, connect the marks, and cut around that outline to make the lining of the bag. You should end up with two lining pieces.

11 Pin the lining pieces right sides together and sew along the two short sides and the bottom, leaving the top open.

12 Turn the raw edges of the unsewn top of the lining over to the wrong side of the lining about 1" and iron flat. Insert the lining (make sure the right sides are facing each other), and pin the folded lining ends in place just under the belt portion of the waistband.

13 Hand-sew your lining in place. (Your sewing machine won't be able to sew over tough spots like the zipper placket and rivets.)

Part 3: Stitching the Straps

In this section, you'll use one of the jean legs you cut off to create straps for your bag, then attach the straps to the body of the bag.

14 Grab one of your jean legs. Cut the seams and the hem off to get two rectangular, single-layered pieces of seamless jean. You will use only one piece for this project. (Put the other one aside to use in another project.) • • • • • • • • • • • • • ▶

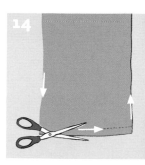

15 Fold your rectangle lengthwise and cut along the fold.

16 You will now have two rectangular strips that you'll be using to make your straps. Take one of these strips, fold it lengthwise with right sides together, and pin. Sew the raw edges of the long side together to make a tube. Turn right side out and iron flat.

17 Repeat with another strip so you have two straps.

18 Turn the raw end of one strap under about ½", then pin it on the inside of the back of the bag, 1" from the side of the bag, and sew it down. If you find a belt loop in the way, remove it so you can sew more easily through the thick layers of the strap and the jeans. • ▶

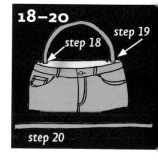

19 Take the other end of the strap, turn it under, and pin it on the back 1" from the other side of the bag; sew it down, again removing belt loops in the way.

20 Repeat on the front of the bag to attach the remaining strap. You can use the strap you just sewed on as your guide for placing the ends of the second strap. Just hold the top of the bag together and mark on the front where the back strap starts and ends. Then, use those marks to guide where you place the front strap.

21 Spice your bag up with a sparkly rhinestone pin, or iron on a patch from your favorite band, then fill up the pockets and head out on the town!

BOOGIE DOWN BELT BAG

Get up on the dance floor, or babysit your bag? Always a tough choice — until now. With the Boogie Down Belt Bag you don't have to worry about a purse cramping your dancing style or having your goods stolen. And losing stuff will be a thing of the past, with your lip gloss, keys, and other necessities all snug in a Velcro-closed pouch right at your hip.

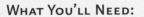

WHAT YOU'LL NEED:

* 1 pair of jeans with back pockets and belt loops

* ½-yard of alternate fabric for lining (a couple of bandannas would work, too)

* 2" Velcro for closure (you can also use a button, snap, or ribbon tie, but the instructions here are for a Velcro closure)

* decorative extras

TIME

DIFFICULTY

Part 1: Cutting the Cloth

Here you'll create the pieces for the body of the bag and the lining.

1 Measure 1" from the outer edges of one back pocket and mark it with chalk in several spots. •

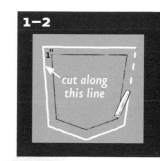

2 Connect the marks to create a 1" chalk "frame" around the pocket. Cut along this line to create the piece you'll use as a pattern for the rest of the bag.

3 Pin the pattern onto one layer of the jean leg. Cut around it to create the same shape. This will make the back of the bag. Put aside.

4 Pin your pattern to two layers of alternate fabric and cut around it to create the same shape. This will make the lining for your bag. Put aside.

Part 2: Making the Flap

Now you will measure and cut the pieces to make the bag's flap.

5 Measure the length of the flat top of your pocket pattern. Mark a straight line of this length on another part of the jean leg. Call this line A. •

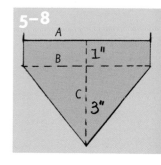

6 From center of line A, measure 1" down, and draw a parallel line below there. Call this line B.

7 From the center of line B, draw a perpendicular line that extends 3" down. Call this line C.

8 From the outer edges of line B, draw two lines that reach to the point at the end of line C.

9 Cut around these lines through one layer of the jean leg and, using this as your pattern piece, cut one piece of your alternate fabric in the same shape. Now you have the two pieces of your flap.

Part 3: Making and Attaching the Loops

You'll turn the belt loops from your jeans into loops for your bag, so it can be attached to your belt.

10 Carefully cut two belt loops from your jeans, keeping the folded, sewn edge of each loop intact.

11 Mark two spots on the bag back about 2" from the top and 2½" from the edges. (They should be 1½" apart.)

12 Pin the belt loops on the bag back so that the top of each belt loop lies along one of the marks you made, and sew the belt loops onto the bag back.

Part 4: Putting the Flap Together

Here you will sew together the flap pieces and attach Velcro for a closure.

13 Pin the flap front and flap lining, right sides together. Sew together, leaving the long top edge open. Turn right side out and use your fingers or a pencil to make sure that you get the corners poked out. • • • • • • • • • • • • • •

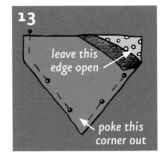

13

leave this edge open

poke this corner out

14 Pin a strip of Velcro to the right side of the flap lining just above the point. Hand sew the Velcro to the flap lining around the Velcro's outer edges. Now your flap is done! • • • • •

14

pin Velcro here

Part 5: Putting It Together

Now you will sew the outer bag together, attach the flap, and attach the outer bag and lining.

15 Pin your bag front and bag back (made out of jean material) with right sides together. Leaving the top open, sew together along the other four outer edges and turn right side out.

16 Pin the flap to the back of the bag only, with right sides of the flap and the bag together.

17 Using a ¼" seam allowance, sew the flap to the bag back.

18 Pin the two lining pieces (made out of alternate fabric) right sides together, leaving about a 2" opening in one of the long sides. Sew, leaving the top and the 2" hole on the side open. •▶

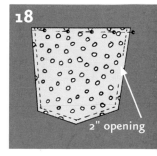

18

2" opening

19 Slip the outer bag into the inside-out lining. Now, if you peek into the top, you'll see the wrong side of the outer bag. • • • • •

20 Match up the side seams and pin the bag and lining together at the top. Then, sew the bag and lining together along the top, where you just pinned.

• • •▶

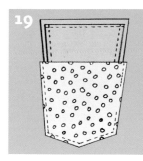

19

21 Put your hand into the 2" opening in the side of the lining (which you created in step 18) and pull out the bag, turning the lining right side out as you go.

22 Pin the hole in the lining shut, sew close to the edge, and push the lining into the bag.

23 Close the flap and mark where the end of the Velcro hits the pocket on the front. Using this as your guide, pin the other piece of Velcro to the pocket and sew around the edge to secure it to the pocket.

24 You're done! Jazz it up a little bit with fabric paint, buttons, pins, or whatever goes best with your ensemble.

STASH YOUR CASH WALLET

I t's a dilemma: You need a new wallet, but the cash it costs to buy one will leave your new wallet empty. With a few scraps of jeans, a zipper, and some fun cotton fabric, you can make yourself this one-of-a-kind cash carrier and still have some money to put in it when you're done!

TIME 🕐🕐🕐

DIFFICULTY 🧵🧵🧵

WHAT YOU'LL NEED:

* 1 jean leg

* one 4" zipper

* ½-yard alternate fabric in a fun pattern (This should be a cotton fabric, not too stretchy or too thick; bandannas could work, too.)

* 1 package ⁷⁄₈" bias tape (which may, but doesn't have to, match the alternate fabric)

* 1 snap (sew-on or press-on)

PART 1: MAKING CHANGE

First, you'll make the outside of the wallet where the zipper change purse will be.

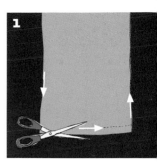

1 Grab one of your jean legs. Cut the seams and the hem off the jean leg to get two rectangular, single-layered pieces of seamless jean. You will use only one piece for this part. (Put the other one aside. You will need it to make the pockets later.)

2 Take your one-layered piece of seamless jean and cut two pieces of jean fabric from it: One should be 5"× 8", and the other one should be 5"× 2".

3 Cut a 5"× 10" piece of cotton fabric.

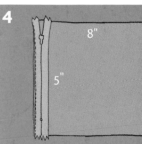

4 Place the zipper face down on the right side of the 5"× 8" jean piece, lining up one long edge of the zipper tape with a short edge of the jean piece.

5 Pin in place and sew, stitching close to the edge of the zipper tape, in between the zipper tape and the zipper teeth. Make sure to sew all the way to the end of the zipper tape, even past where the zipper begins to unzip. It will be easier to sew on the zipper if you start at the top and stitch the first few inches with the zipper closed, then open the zipper, drawing it past where you've already sewn it down.

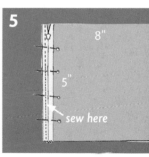

sew here

6 Open the seam (so the zipper and jeans are right side up) and iron flat the new seam between the zipper tape and jean edge.

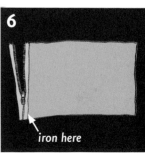

iron here

7 Pin the other long side of the zipper to the long edge of the 5"× 2" piece of jeans fabric. Repeat steps 4–5.

8 You now have a single piece joined by the zipper that measures roughly 5"× 10". • • • • • • • • • • • • • • • • • • •▶

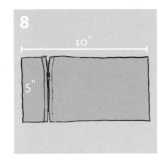

9 Place the alternate fabric wrong side up on your work surface and lay your jean piece on top of it, right side up. (They will be wrong sides together.) Pin them together along all of the edges.

10 Keeping the jean fabric on top, fold the rectangle in half until the two short edges meet. Draw a line down the center of the fold on the jeans side. • • • • • • • • • • • • • • • • • • •▶

11 Sew the layers together along this center line.

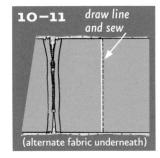

PART 2: WHERE THE STUFF GOES

Now you will make the interior pockets of the wallet: a long pocket for cash, and several smaller, divided pockets for your ID and other cards. You will cut three pieces of fabric for the pockets, then hem the top of each of them.

12 Grab the other one-layered rectangle of seamless jean left over from Part 1. From this piece, cut one rectangle of jean leg that is 10"× 5".

13 Take the alternate fabric and cut one rectangle that is 10"× 4" and one rectangle that is 10"× 3".

14 To hem, lay the 10"× 5" piece of jean leg right side down and fold one long edge over to the wrong side ½". Iron, pin into place, and stitch down close to the raw edge. Repeat on remaining two alternate fabric pieces. Now you have three pocket pieces.

15 Place the jeans pocket piece right side up on your work surface.

16 Place the larger alternate fabric pocket piece on top, right side up, matching raw bottom edges and corners. • • • • • • • • • • ▶

17 Place the smaller alternate fabric pocket piece on top of these two layers, also right side up, matching up raw bottom edge and corners with the preceeding layers.

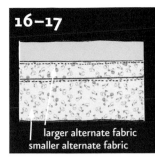

16–17

larger alternate fabric
smaller alternate fabric

18 Pin these three layers together around all sides. • • • • • • • • • •

19 With the alternate fabric pockets facing up, using your ruler, draw a straight perpendicular line down the middle of the three layers.

20 Sew along this line to attach the three layers together and create divided card pockets.

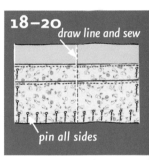

18–20
draw line and sew

pin all sides

PART 3: PUTTING IT ALL TOGETHER

Here you'll join the change purse and card pockets together.

21 Place the outer wallet, with the zipper, on your work surface so that the alternate fabric is facing you.

22 Place the inside pocket piece, layered alternate fabric side facing up, on top of the outer wallet, matching bottom edges and corners. Your stitched center lines should more or less line up as well.

23 Fold your bias tape in half lengthwise around the raw edges of all layers of fabric. You are binding the layers together by sandwiching them between the halves of the bias tape.

24 Pin the bias tape and fabric together. Don't worry if there are a few wrinkles in the bias tape, as long as it continues to enfold all of the layers of fabric. • • • • • • • • • • • •

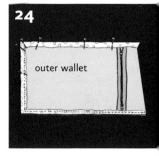

24

outer wallet

25 Continue folding and pinning until you reach the point where you started. Leave 1" extra of bias tape, then cut off your bias tape. Fold the raw edge of the bias tape under, then in half the other way, to enfold the layers of fabric within it as you did with the rest. • • • • • • • • • • • • • • • • ▶

25   1" extra of bias tape

26 Sew the bias tape and layers of fabric together, stitching close to the raw edge of the bias tape.

PART 4: MAKE IT SNAPPY

Now that the wallet is all together, you'll want to be able to keep it closed — with your snap.

27 With the interior pockets of the wallet facing up, make a mark in the center of one short edge, ½" away from the bias binding. (The mark will be on a pocket, and that is OK.)

28 Make a corresponding mark on the other short edge. (This will also be on a pocket, which is also fine.)

29 Sew or hammer your snap, fastening pieces to their corresponding marks on the fabric.

30 Pop in your cash, zip in your change, slip in your cards, and go!

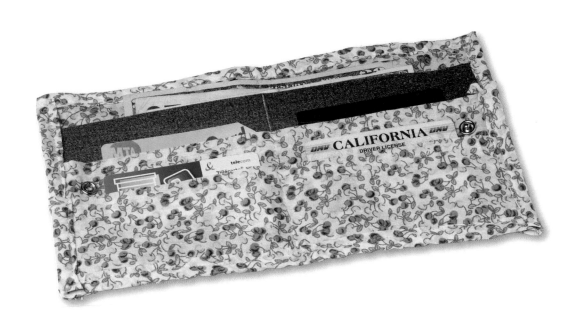

BLUE JEAN BLACK MARKET

Before the fall of Communism in Eastern Europe, American blue jeans were strictly forbidden. They symbolized free-wheeling capitalism and so were considered contraband in the USSR. This, of course, meant that they were seriously in demand! American brands of blue jeans sold for incredible prices on the black market to fashion-forward Soviet teens who wanted a taste of life on the other side of the Wall.

MULTIPURPOSE WRITE-ON PENCIL POUCH

Pencil cases aren't just for pencils anymore. You can use them for pens, lip gloss, wrapped candies, keys, and, of course, that-time-of-the-month supplies. You can even put small or delicate gifts in them, instead of using standard gift bags or wrapping paper. And once you get the hang of sewing in a zipper, these dandy little pouches are ridiculously easy to make. Want to make your pouch easy to transport? Add a ribbon or rope handle to transform it into a clutch and take it on the road.

TIME 🕐🕐

DIFFICULTY 🧵

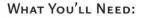

WHAT YOU'LL NEED:

* 1 jean leg

* 18" length of ribbon that color coordinates with the zipper

* 9" zipper in a fun color (Note: This pouch has a 9" zipper, but any length you like will do. Smaller ones are good for smaller items. Just be sure to cut your fabric an inch longer than the zipper length so you don't end up sewing across the zipper teeth on the ends.)

* decorative extras

PART 1: MAKING THE "BUTTERFLY" BODY

You will attach two pieces of denim by sewing a zipper in between them to make a shape of a butterfly.

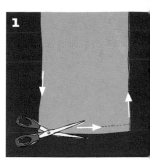

1 Grab one of your jean legs. Cut the seams and the hem off to get two rectangular, single-layered pieces of seamless jean. Cut two 7"×10" rectangles from these two layers. • • • • • • • • •

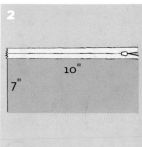

2 Place the zipper face down on the right side of a 7"×10" rectangle, matching one long edge of the zipper tape with with one long edge of the rectangle. • • • • • • • • • • • • • • • • • • ▶

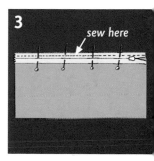

3 Pin the zipper in place and sew, stitching between the zipper tape and the teeth. Make sure to sew all the way to the end of the tape, even past where the zipper begins to unzip. It will be easier to sew on the zipper if you start at the top and stitch the first few inches with the zipper closed, then open it, drawing it past where you've already sewn it down. • • • • • • • ▶

4 Open the seam (so the zipper and jeans are right side up) and iron flat the new seam between the zipper tape and the jean edge. •

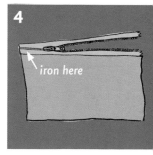

iron here

5 Pin the other long side of the zipper to the long edge of the remaining jeans rectangle. Repeat steps 3–4 on this side. • • •▶

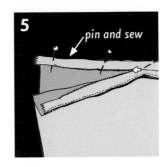

6 With both seams opened, you should now have what looks like a butterfly with denim wings and a zipper down the middle. •

Part 2: Making the Pouch Portable

To make your zipper pouch into a clutch, you'll attach a loop of ribbon to act as a handle.

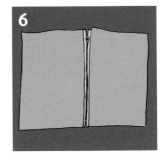

7 Take your ribbon and fold it in half to make a loop. • • • • •

8 Place the two raw edges of the folded ribbon on the right side of one of the rectangles, on a short side and about 2" away from the zipper.

9 Pin the ribbon in place and sew it to the denim using a ¼" seam allowance. • • •▶

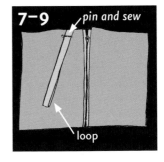

Part 3: Turning Your Butterfly Into a Pouch

You'll sew together the sides of the pouch to finish it off.

10 This gets its own step because it is very important: Unzip the zipper! You will later turn the case right side out through the opening left by the zipper.

11 Fold the "butterfly" in half, right sides together. The open zipper will be the fold.

12 Line up the corners and pin the three non-zipper sides of denim together.

13 Starting with one end of the zipper, stitch the case together down one short side, across the bottom long edge, and up the last short side. Sew across the zipper tape just as you do the jean fabric.

14 Turn the bag right side out through the opening created by the open zipper.

15 Decorate as you please. Then, pop in your pens, pencils, lip gloss, or whatever else needs carrying, zip up and go.

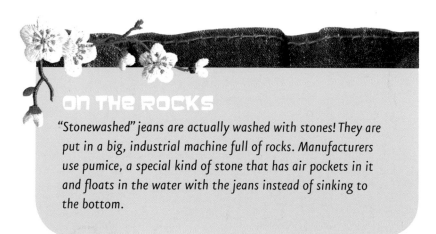

ON THE ROCKS

"Stonewashed" jeans are actually washed with stones! They are put in a big, industrial machine full of rocks. Manufacturers use pumice, a special kind of stone that has air pockets in it and floats in the water with the jeans instead of sinking to the bottom.

waist not, want not belt

Everyone wears belts with jeans. But have you ever worn jeans as a belt? Denim is a great material for a belt because it is durable, matches with everything, and can give a girlish outfit (think: flowered dress) a tougher look. Cinch your favorite dress, skirt, or flowing top with comfort, ease, and an indiscernable jeans chic.

TIME

DIFFICULTY

Part 1: Taking Measurements

You'll get the measurements for your new belt.

1 Measure around your waist or below your waist, wherever you would like the belt to cinch.

2 Add 6" to this measurement and you have the length of your belt. Write this down as length.

3 Measure the rod that crosses the center of your belt buckle.

4 Add 1" to this measurement. Write this down as width.

Part 2: Cutting the Cloth

Here you'll cut out the material you need for your belt.

Important: If the inseam of your jeans is equal to or greater than your belt's length, you can skip this part, take your jean leg, and go straight to Part 3. If the inseam is less than the length of the belt, you will need more material and must follow steps 5–7 below.

5 Grab your jean leg. Cut the seams and the hem off to get two rectangular, single-layered pieces of seamless jean. · · · · · · · · · ▶

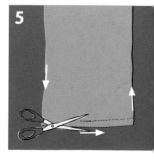

6 To create one long leg from which to cut your belt, string the two pieces of denim together, pinning then sewing them along their short sides; leave a ½" seam allowance.

7 Iron this seam nice and flat.

Part 3: Drawing Out Your Belt

Using the measurements from Part 1, and the piece of jean (from either Part 1 or Part 2), you will draw your belt and cut it out.

8 Draw a rectangle on the jeans fabric that is 3" wide and the length of the waist measurement you wrote down in step 2. You should leave at least 2½" of free space from the short edges.

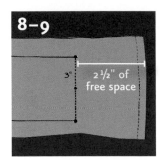

9 You want the end of your belt to have a point. To make this point, find the center of one short side of the rectangle and mark this spot.

10 Measure 2" away from this spot (outside of the rectangle) and make another mark.

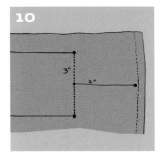

11 Using your ruler, draw a line from one corner of the short side of the rectangle to the mark you made in step 10.

12 To finish the point at the end of your belt, draw another line from the other corner of the short side of the rectangle that also meets the mark from step 10.

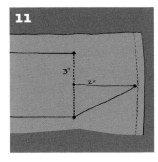

Part 4: Cutting Out Your Belt

You'll cut out the material you need for your belt. You will be cutting it out from either the original, still intact jean leg (cut only one layer!) or from the longer piece of jean material you made in Part 2.

13 Cut along the lines that you drew to create a long belt piece with one straight end and one pointed end.

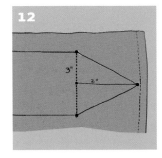

14 Pin this piece to your alternate fabric, right sides together.

15 Using the jean piece as a pattern, cut around it to create the fabric back of your belt.

PART 5: SEWING THE BELT TOGETHER

Now that you have your belt pieces, you'll sew together the front and the back.

16 The jean piece and fabric piece should still be pinned, right sides together.

17 Leaving ½" all around for the seams, sew the pieces together. Start at the beginning of one long edge. Then, when you reach the pointy end of the belt, leave your needle in the fabric, and turn the fabric so that you can start sewing down the other side. This will allow you to have a nice sharp point. Sew down the other long side, leaving the straight, short edge open.

18 Clip the corners away from the three points at the end of the belt so it will turn out with nice crisp corners. • • • • • • • • • • ▶

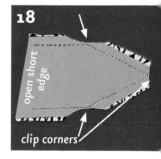

19 Turn the belt right side out through the short edge you left open.

20 Using a pencil, poke out the pointed end of the belt, and iron so that both layers of the belt lie flat.

Part 6: Buckling Up

You'll attach the buckle and sew it in place.

21 Tuck ½" of raw edges, from the open short edge of the belt, inside the belt. Iron this short edge flat so that the raw edges stay inside.

22 Run the short edge up and over the middle rod of the belt buckle, pulling about 2" through. • • • • • • • • • • • • • ▶

22

23 Turn the open edge under ½" and pin to the fabric side of your belt. •

24 Sew, where the folded short edge meets the belt, to secure the buckle to the belt. • • • ▶

23–24

pin and sew here

25 Cinch around your favorite top or dress!

naVIGaTe THe Jean SHOPPING JUNGLe

With so many brands, washes, and cuts, jean stores can be a jungle. Here are a few tips to keep your sanity in the dressing room and ensure that you are making good purchases:

1 Sit, bend, and move around to see that the jeans don't gape, squeeze, dip, or anything else that would make them uncomfortable or embarrassing in normal life.

2 Remember that if the jeans contain spandex (check the label), they are likely to stretch out with regular wear. So if you are between sizes, go for the smaller one.

3 Even though many jeans are sized in inches, fit still varies between brands and styles. If you're trying on an unfamiliar brand, grab the sizes just below and above your "usual" before you head into the dressing room to save time.

4 Most jeans are cut longer than the average girl's leg these days. Make sure you bring shoes with a heel the height you usually wear, and roll the hem under to the length you will hem it to so that you can accurately judge the look of the jeans as you'll wear them.

5 Twirl and look in the mirror from every angle — especially the back! Sometimes jeans that look good from the front do little or nothing for your other assets.

SPICY SLIPPERS

I s the floor too hard and cold for your sensitive tootsies during winter? Just like a hot bowl of chili heats up your belly on a cold night, these spicy slippers will keep your soles warm and cozy when the ground below feels less than welcoming.

TIME

DIFFICULTY

What You'll Need:

* 1 jean leg

* your favorite flip-flops

* newsprint or other large sheet of paper

* pen or marker

* ½-yard alternate fabric (Choose a washable fabric, since these are going on your feet and the floor!)

* ½-yard batting

* 1 package ⁷/₈" bias tape

Part 1: Designing Your Sole

Using your flip-flops as a model, you'll create a paper pattern for the soles of your slippers.

1 Place one of your flip-flops, sole down, on a piece of newsprint or large paper.

2 Trace around the flip-flop, as close as you can to the edges. When you take the flip-flop away, there will be an outline roughly the shape and size of the sole.

3 Measure ½" away from the outline, making marks around the entire outline and then connecting them. At this point, you should have one shoe print the exact size of your flip-flop and a second shoe print around it ½" larger.

4 Cut out the larger shoe print to make a paper pattern for the sole of your slippers.

Part 2: Cutting Out Your Sole

Using the paper pattern, you'll cut six slipper sole pieces: two from the jean leg, two from the alternate fabric and two from the batting.

5 With the jean leg still intact, pin your pattern piece to both layers of denim and cut around it. When you unpin the pattern piece and place the pieces you've cut right sides down, you'll notice that you've made denim slipper soles for both your right and left feet. • ▶

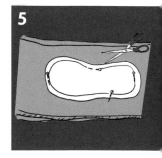

6 Now fold a piece of your alternate fabric in half, right sides together.

7 Pin the paper pattern to the alternate fabric and cut around it to make the footbed of your slippers.

8 Fold a piece of batting in half and pin the paper pattern to it.

9 Cut around the pattern through both layers of batting. This will give you stuffing to make your slippers nice and cushy.

PART 3: IT'S A STRAP!

You'll make some sturdy straps for your new comfy slippers.

10 Measure across the top of your foot, at the widest part. This should be from roughly below your big toe across to the spot below your pinkie toe. Write down this measurement. Call it **W**.

11 Cut a piece of jean leg that measures 3" × **W**. This will be your strap. • ▶

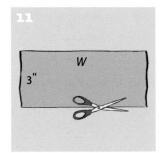

11

12 Using this piece as a pattern for your strap, cut another piece out of denim and two more out of the alternate fabric.

13 Using these, pin one jean piece and one alternate fabric piece along the edge that measured the width of your foot (the **W** side), right sides together.

14 Sew across both the **W** side edges, leaving the shorter ends open. (These will later be attached to the slipper.)

15 Turn it right side out through one of the openings and iron it flat.

16 Repeat with the other piece of denim and alternate fabric to make the second strap.

Part 4: You're a Shoe-In

Here, you'll put all the parts together.

17 Place one jean slipper sole wrong side up on your work surface. Place the batting on top of it, then the alternate fabric on top of the batting, right side up.

18 Pin the open edges of the slipper strap onto the sandwiched layers of denim, batting, and alternate fabric, positioning the slipper strap as you see it in the photograph of the finished slippers. • ▶

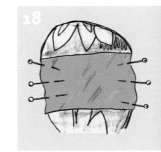

19 Sewing as close as you can to the edge, stitch the strap to all three layers of your slipper sole. (The rough edges of the strap are left out here; they will be bound by bias tape later on.)

Part 5: Binding This Baby

Because you have so many layers of fabric, you'll bind the edges of the slipper with bias tape.

20 Fold your bias tape in half lengthwise, sandwiching the layers of denim, batting, and alternate fabric (as well as the slipper strap) between the two halves of tape. • • • • • • • • • • • • • ▶

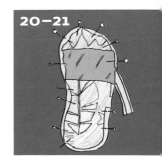

21 Continue around the circumference of the slippers, folding the tape around the layers and pinning every so often. It is better to over-pin in this case to keep everything in line.

22 When you get to where you started, overlap the beginning of the bias tape with the end by about ½".

23 Sew the bias tape, alternate fabric, denim, and batting together, stitching close to the non-folded edge of the bias tape.

24 Repeat steps 17–23 to make your second slipper.

25 Slide on your slippers and swan around the house!

GET YOUR GLITTER ON EARRINGS

These bold hoops are not for the fashionably faint of heart. A little bit bohemian, a little bit rock and roll, they are sure to make you stand out in the crowd. For the hippest look possible, wear them with black jeans, a white tank top, a few choice bangles, and a whole lot of attitude.

WHAT YOU'LL NEED:

* 2 double-stitched jean seams (each about 7" in length)

* two 24-gauge gold-tone wires (each about 2½" in length)

* 1 pair gold fishhook pierced-ear wires

* 10–20 small beads with holes large enough that they can be strung on the gold wire

TIME 🕐

DIFFICULTY 🧵

PART 1: SHOOTING HOOPS

You will design the hoops of your earrings.

1 Take one of your double-stitched jean seams (7" in length) and form it into a circle, overlapping one short edge of the seam with the other by ½".

2 Stitch it in place to secure a circle.

3 Take one of your 2½" wires and fold in half to make a loop.

4 Put the loop end through the inside of the jean circle.

5 Run the wire ends through the loop to secure the wire around jean circle.

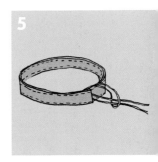

6 Pull the ends through the loop until all that is left of the loop is ¼" of wire. Twist the loop around itself to secure.

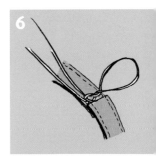

7 Separate the tails of the wire and begin wrapping one around the jean circle. Thread a bead on the wire for every other loop. Continue wrapping until you reach the end of the wire, which should also be the center bottom (middle) of the jean circle.

8 Repeat step 7 with second tail of wire, going in the other direction, to wrap the second half of the jean circle in beads and wire.

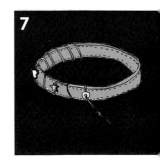

9 Twist the ends of the wire tails together and press them flat against the inside of the jean circle to secure.

Part 2: Making Them Hang

You will attach your new hoops to the ear wires to finish them off.

10 Take one of your fishhook wires. Find the small closed circle at the bottom and the tiny gap in the closed circle and gently pull it apart until it opens slightly. · · · · · · · · · · · · · ▶

11 Slide loop of wire on denim earring into the loop of wire at the bottom of the fishhook. Then press the fishhook loop shut again. ·

12 Put on your earrings and rock the house!

· · · · · ▶

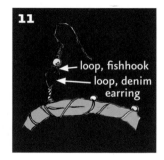

loop, fishhook
loop, denim earring

BLUE JEANS: A CELEBRITY TREND

Blue jeans really took off as a fashion trend thanks to the celebrities of the 1950s. Once hot stars like Marilyn Monroe, James Dean, and Marlon Brando were photographed off-set in jeans, the attire became leisure clothing must-haves for all fashion followers. Today, celebrities are still true to their blues — pick up any glossy magazine and you'll see stars in some of the hottest jean brands.

CUFF 'em BRACELET

There's no question that cuff bracelets are cool — but it's always a challenge to find one that fits just right. Either they squeeze off your circulation, or hang loose and limp from your wrist. This piece of jean jewelry is the solution to the perennial cuff bracelet problem. It works because you use the measurements of your very own wrist to create a made-to-order bracelet that will fit exactly as you please and wow all of the fashionistas in your life.

WHAT YOU'LL NEED:

* 1 scrap of jean fabric long enough to circle your wrist and at least 4" wide

* 2 sew-on or hammer-on pressure snaps

* decorative extras

TIME

DIFFICULTY

Part 1: Measuring Up

You will measure your wrist to cut a custom-fit jean piece to make the cuff, then hem the long sides.

1 Using a measuring tape, measure around the smallest part of your wrist. Add 1" to this number and write it down.

2 Cut out a piece of jean that is 4" wide and the length of your measurement from step 1. Fold the long raw edges to the wrong side ½". Pin in place.

3 Sew the pinned-down edges close to the fold using contrasting thread and a decorative stitch to give the bracelet a little oomph. •▶

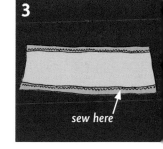

sew here

Part 2: Snapping Up

You'll attach snaps so the cuff fits snugly.

4 Turn the jean piece wrong side up. Find the raw edges now on the ends of the bracelet. Attach the protruding part of one snap (often called the "male" section of the snap on the package directions) to one of the raw edges, ½" away from the raw edge and ¼" from the long sewn edge. Attach the snap on the wrong side. Attach the protruding part of the other snap also ½" away from the raw edge and ¼" from the other sewn edge, on the wrong side.

5 Wrap the cuff around your wrist, overlapping snaps with the other raw short end of the bracelet.

6 Adjust overlap until cuff fits as you would like it to. Then make marks where the snap protrusions hit the bracelet.

7 Attach the second, or "female," part of the snaps to correspond with the marks you just made and create the perfect fit. Trim away any excess cuff that protrudes past the snaps, leaving the edges raw. •

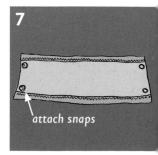

attach snaps

8 Embellish your cuff with buttons, embroidery, or 1" pins from your favorite bands and marvel at your new tough cuff.

GARDEN BLUES FLOWER CHOKER

Fabric flower pins are always cool. Stylish girls sport them on everything, from jackets and pants to hats and scarves. And if flower pins are hot, then chokers are even hotter. This project combines a denim flower pin with a chic tie-on choker to make a versatile fashion statement that will take you from garden to urban and back again.

TIME

DIFFICULTY

WHAT YOU'LL NEED:

FOR FLOWER PIN

* 2 scraps jean fabric, at least 4"× 4" each

* small amount of polyester stuffing

* 2 yards brightly colored embroidery floss

* 3 tapestry or upholstery needles

* 1" sew-on pin backing

FOR CHOKER

* 1 piece jean leg, at least 2" wide and long enough to wrap around your throat once

* 2' of 1" wide grosgrain ribbon

PART 1: FLOWER POWER

To make the flower for your choker, you will sew two circles of denim together, stuff them, and embellish with embroidery floss.

1 Cut out two circles of denim, each 3½" in diameter. If you have trouble cutting an even circle, try tracing the mouth of a drinking glass.

2 Pin the circles, right sides together.

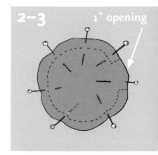

3 Sew around the circumference of the circles using a ½" seam allowance. Leave a 1" opening for turning right side out and stuffing.

4 Turn it right side out through the hole.

5 Push stuffing into the circle through the opening until the circle is moderately stuffed.

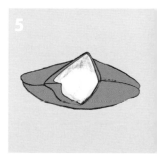

6 Turn the raw edges of the opening inside the circle and hand sew it closed using small stitches.

7 Thread your tapestry or upholstery needle with brightly colored embroidery floss that has been knotted at the end.

8 Push your needle through the center of the circle.

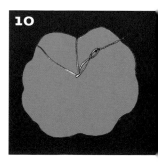

9 Wrap the floss around the edge of the circle and push the needle back through the center. Pull tightly so that the floss indents the circle.

10 Wrap the floss around again, this time about 1" from the previous stitch, and push the needle through the center, pulling tight to form your first "petal."

11 Continue in this manner until you have made six evenly spaced petals separated by bright floss. End with the needle coming out of the center of the top of the flower. · · · · · · · · ▶

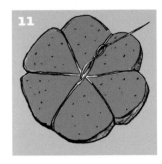

12 String a small button on to the floss and sew it to the center of the flower. ·

13 Knot the floss at the back of the flower (where the original knot at the end of your floss is) and trim floss ends.

14 Sew the pin backing to the back of the flower. · · · ▶

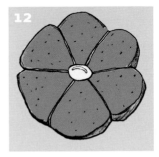

15 You can go ahead and pin your flower to your favorite clothes, or continue below to make it into a flower choker.

PART 2: MAKING THE CHOKER

You will cut and hem a piece of jean fabric to fit your neck. Then you'll attach ribbons for a flirty choker closure.

16 Measure around your neck. Add 1" to this measurement. Write it down.

17 Cut a length of jean fabric 2" wide and the length of the measurement you wrote down in step 16.

18 Fold the short edges of the rectangle in ½" and pin in place.

19 Sew the folded edges down close to the raw edges.

20 Pin the end of one length of ribbon to the center of one short edge of the denim, with an overlap of about ½".

21 Fold both long edges of the denim rectangle to the wrong side until they meet in the center, wrapping around the ribbon at the short edge, and pin. ························▶

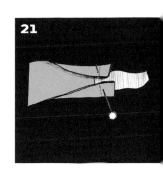

21

22 Sew your ribbon in place along the line of stitching you made when hemming the short edge.

23 Repeat with the second length of ribbon on the second short edge.

24 Pin the remainder of the long edges of denim so that they lie folded in, meeting at the center.

25 Sew the edges down, close to the fold, all along the pinned long edges. Iron flat.

26 Pin your flower to the choker at a jaunty angle and tie the ribbons at the back of your neck for a new take on old-fashioned glamour.

Jeans Climb the Social Ladder

For the first 50 years of their existence, blue jeans were strictly blue collar — for mining, ranching, and other hard work. But the advent of the Hollywood Western in the 1930s changed all that. Visions of the big stars playing cowboys had Americans booking dude ranch vacations and rushing to buy their own pair of bad boy blue jeans.

BLUES YOU CAN USE

IN*JEAN*IOUS GIFTS AND
FUN THINGS FOR THE HOUSE

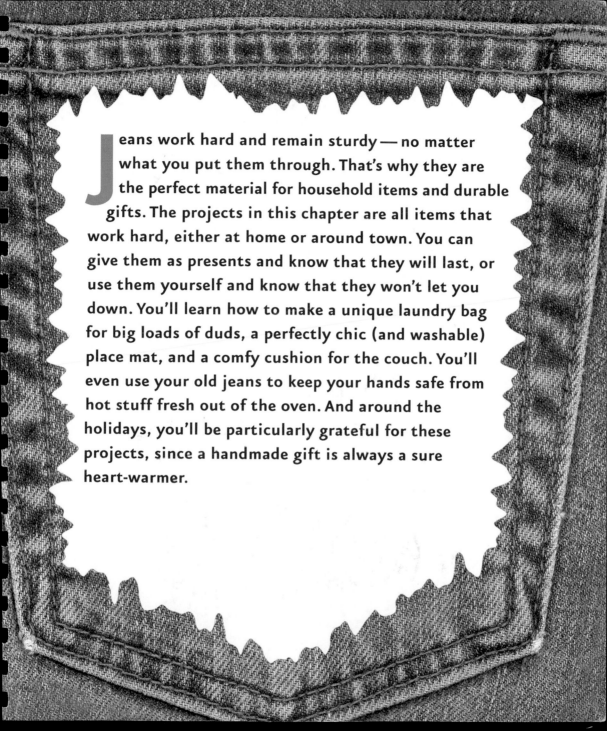

Jeans work hard and remain sturdy — no matter what you put them through. That's why they are the perfect material for household items and durable gifts. The projects in this chapter are all items that work hard, either at home or around town. You can give them as presents and know that they will last, or use them yourself and know that they won't let you down. You'll learn how to make a unique laundry bag for big loads of duds, a perfectly chic (and washable) place mat, and a comfy cushion for the couch. You'll even use your old jeans to keep your hands safe from hot stuff fresh out of the oven. And around the holidays, you'll be particularly grateful for these projects, since a handmade gift is always a sure heart-warmer.

SUDS YOUR DUDS LAUNDRY BAG

You know that chair in the corner of your room? News flash: It's not a laundry bag. And that canvas bag stashed in your closet that you're supposed to be using for laundry? It's looking kind of dull. (Hey, maybe that's why you never use it!)

You've got cool clothes. You need a cool place to put them when they are dirty. With one old pair of jeans, you can make a stylish and functional place to stash your dirty duds until you find the time to wash them. And in addition to cool, you get the added bonus of practical: The pockets on the jeans are the perfect place to keep change and a packet of detergent if you need to haul everything to the local laundromat.

TIME 🕐

DIFFICULTY 🧵

WHAT YOU'LL NEED:

* 1 pair of jeans (wide-legged work best if you want a roomy bag)

* 3 yards of bright ribbon for a drawstring

Part 1: From Slacks to Sack

You'll cut the jean legs apart at the inner seam and make the jeans into a tube.

1 Starting at the bottom of one leg and keeping close to the inner seams of the jean legs, cut all the way up one leg, across the center seam and down the other leg. When you are finished, the legs will be held together only by the outer seams.

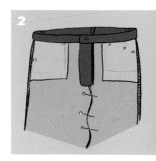

cut here ↗

2 Turn your jeans inside out and pin the raw edges of the front of the legs together. Sew these raw edges together from just below the zipper to the hem.

3 Pin the raw edges of the back of the legs together and sew as you did for the front.

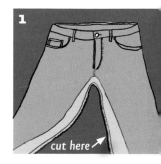

Part 2: Bottoming Out

You'll trim away the excess jean fabric, then sew up the bottom of the bag.

4 Turn your tube right side out.

5 Cut off enough of the bottom of the tube so that it measures 3' from top to bottom when you are done cutting.

6 Turn the tube inside out again and pin the raw edges at the bottom of the tube together and stitch across using a ½" seam allowance.

7 Turn right side out, thread your ribbon through the belt loops, and get washing!

CORDON "BLUE" PLACE MAT

"**P**lace mat" and "creative" are words that don't often appear in the same sentence. But add a few scraps of blue jeans to your table settings and you might start to think differently. These delish place mats, a scrumptious dinner, and a group of good pals are the perfect ingredients for a real Cordon "Blue" dinner party.

WHAT YOU'LL NEED:

* enough jean scraps to make 17 strips of denim that measure 13" long and 2" wide (different colors and shades are fine)

* ½-yard alternate fabric (A heavy, machine-washable cotton fabric is best; canvas or any heavy-weight cotton works well.)

TIME

DIFFICULTY

Part 1: Making Strips and Stripes

You'll sew strips of jean scraps together into a single striped piece that will serve as the top of the place mat.

1 Cut 17 strips of denim that measure 13" long and 2" wide.

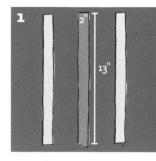

2 Place the strips on your table in a row. Put them in an order that is pleasing to the eye. If you are using denim from a few different pairs of jeans, this is a good time to get creative with making a pattern using the different shades.

3 When you are satisfied with your arrangement of strips, mark each one with a number in the upper right hand corner, from 1 through 17.

4 Place strip 1 on your work surface right side up.

5 Place strip 2 on top of strip 1, right side down. (Strip 1 and 2 should be right sides together.)

6 Pin them together along one of the long edges, and stitch using a ½" seam allowance.

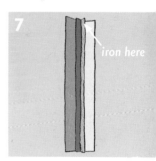

7 Open the strips out so that the wrong side is facing you and iron the seam you just sewed.

8 Place this sewn-together strip right side up on your work surface. Place strip 3 on it right side down, matching up one of the long edges of strip 3 with the raw edge of strip 2.

9 Pin in place along this edge and sew using a ½" seam allowance.

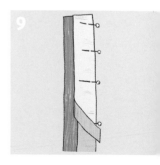

10 Open up this new three-strip piece wrong side up and iron the seam you just sewed.

11 Continue in this fashion until you have no more strips to sew.

12 You will have a single piece of sewn strips that measures roughly 13"× 18½". · · · · · · · · · · · · · · · · · · · ▷

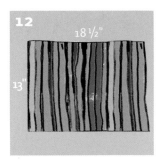

PART 2: BACKING IT UP

You'll use your alternate fabric to add a designer backing to the place mat.

13 Cut a piece of your alternate fabric that measures 13"× 18½".

14 Pin the rectangle of jean strips on top of the alternate fabric rectangle, right sides together. · · · · · · · · · ▷

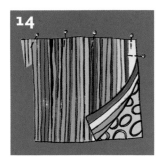

15 Leaving a 4" opening on one short edge (for turning the place mat right side out later on), sew all four sides together using a ½" seam allowance. · · · · · · · · · · · ▷

16 Clip the corners so that you get nice points when you turn it right side out. · · · · · · · · · · · · · · · · · ·

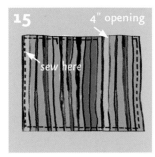

17 Turn your place mat right side out through the small hole in the side.

18 Tuck the raw edges of the hole inside the place mat ½" and pin shut.

· · · · · ▷

19 Starting with the pinned edge, sew all the way around the place mat using a ½" seam allowance. Use a contrasting color thread so that this second seam sewn on the top of the place mat both closes the turning hole and provides a decorative border.

20 Make more! Once you've learned this technique, you can use different sized strips in different arrangements, and even mix and match denim with other fabrics to create an ultra-modern, funky-looking dinner table.

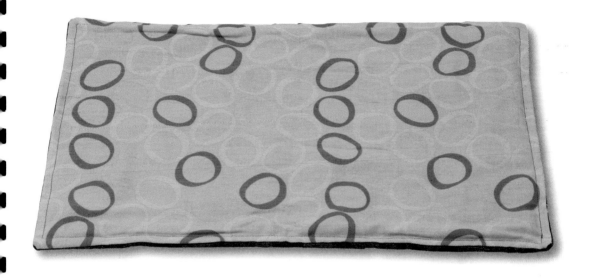

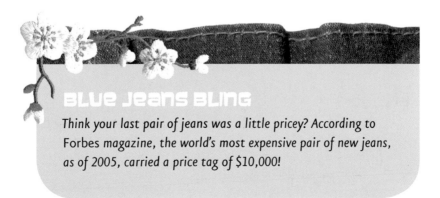

BLUE JEANS BLING

Think your last pair of jeans was a little pricey? According to Forbes magazine, the world's most expensive pair of new jeans, as of 2005, carried a price tag of $10,000!

CRAFTY COASTERS

A lot of people get pretty steamed up about rings on their nice wood furniture. But let's face it—coasters are blah. Usually made out of tacky plastic or poorly painted wood, they are better left inside the drawer where they typically get stashed. You'll be glad to know that these jean coasters are anything but standard. They are a mix of denim, fun patterns, and cool geometric shapes. They're so pretty, you'll actually want to use them. And that makes for a happy you, and a happy table.

What You'll Need:

* 2 jean scraps measuring at least 5"× 5" for each coaster

* ½-yard heavyweight alternate fabric in a fun pattern

* ½-yard batting

TIME

DIFFICULTY

PART 1: CUTTING THE CLOTH

You'll make square and triangular pieces for your part-jean, part-fabric coasters.

1 Cut one square of denim 5"× 5". • ▶

2 Cut another square of denim 5½"× 5½".

3 Cut one square of batting 5"× 5".

4 Cut a square of alternate fabric 5½" × 5½".

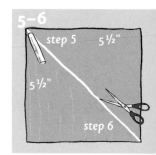

5 Using your ruler, draw a straight line diagonally across the 5½"× 5½" square of denim. • ▶

6 Cut along this line to create two denim triangles.

7 Repeat steps 5 and 6 with the alternate fabric square measuring 5½"× 5½"

PART 2: COASTING THROUGH

You'll sew your pieces together to make a patchwork-looking coaster with a cushy middle.

8 Place one jean triangle on top of one alternate fabric triangle, right sides together.

9 Pin the fabric together at the long diagonal edge and sew here, using a ½" seam allowance.

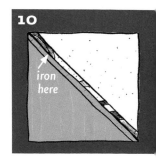

10 Flatten it out with the wrong side up and iron the seam open. • ▶

11 Turn the piece right side up and trim any seam allowance that pokes out from underneath at the corners so that the sewn-together triangles make a neat square.

12 Place the batting on your work surface, and place the sewn-together square right side up on top of the batting, then place the 5"× 5" jean square on top, right side down. • • • • •▶

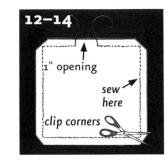

13 Pin these layers together and sew with ½" seam allowance, leaving a 1" opening in one side (for turning inside out later on).

14 Clip the corners so the points turn out neatly.

15 Turn right side out through hole on the side.

16 Tuck the raw edges inside the hole ½" and pin hole closed.

17 Sew around the entire perimeter of the coaster using a ¼" seam allowance. For a bit of contrast, use a brightly colored thread. If you like, use fabric paint or embroidery thread to decorate the all-jean side with words or designs.

18 Pour yourself a cold iced tea, lemonade, or soda and put it down on your new coaster!

TOAST YOUR NEW COASTERS

Now that you have something to rest your drink on, you'll need something to drink! Nothing tastes better on a hot day than something tangy, sweet, and sparkling.

Long Cool Limeade

2 tablespoons frozen limeade concentrate

8 ounces sparkling water or club soda

ice cubes

Place ice in your favorite glass. Drizzle the limeade concentrate over the ice. Pour seltzer in to fill the glass. Sip and enjoy!

HOT STUFF POT HOLDER

Every girl's been burned by love. And we all know that an adorable pair of jeans makes great armor when facing an old flame. But just because those once-perfect jeans have stopped giving you that "I can take on the world!" feeling, you don't have to put them out to pasture. Let them keep on protecting you by refashioning them into a cute pot holder. That way, they can continue helping you stay safe and cool in the hottest of situations.

WHAT YOU'LL NEED:

* 1 jean leg
* 1 pot holder
* 1 sheet of newsprint or other large paper
* 1 pen or marker
* ½-yard batting
* 1 package ⅞" bias tape

TIME

DIFFICULTY

PART 1: PLOTTING OUT YOUR POT HOLDER

You'll trace your pattern and cut out your pot holder pieces.

1 Place your pot holder on a sheet of newsprint or paper.

2 Trace around pot holder with a pen to create an outline on the paper.

3 Try on the pot holder you just traced. If you think it is a bit too large, then your outline will work fine. Don't draw any more. If you think it fits just right, then you need to make a bigger outline, so make a second outline ½" around the original.

4 Cut around the last line you drew to create your pot holder pattern.

5 Fold your intact jean leg in half, short sides together.

6 Pin the pattern piece to all four layers of the jean leg.

7 Cut around the pattern piece to create four identical pieces of pot holder-shaped denim.

8 Pin the pattern piece to three layers of batting and cut around it to create three pieces of pot holder-shaped batting.

Part 2: Heat-Proofing Your Holder

For better heat resistance, you'll sandwich two layers of batting between two layers of denim and then quilt them together in a cross-hatch pattern to make the bottom of the pot holder.

9 Sandwich two layers of batting between two denim pieces, wrong sides together.

10 Starting ½" away from the top rounded edge of the potholder, draw a straight, horizontal line across the width of the top layer of denim. • ▶

11 Draw another line 1" below your first line, and continue drawing lines 1" apart until you reach the bottom of the pot holder.

12 Starting ½" from the tip of the thumb, draw a vertical line that is perpendicular to the first set of lines you drew.

13 Measure 1" away from this line and draw another, continuing in this manner until you have cross-hatched lines covering this top layer of denim.

14 Pin together the two layers of denim, sandwiching the • • ▶
two layers of batting between them. • • • • • • • • • • • •

15 Using a bright, contrasting color thread, sew all layers together following each of the two sets of parallel lines you drew. The stitching should make a cross-hatch pattern on the fabric. The end result is the bottom of your pot holder. • • • • • ▶

sew along cross-hatched lines ⟶

Part 3: Fits Like a Glove

You'll now sew together the quilted pot holder bottom to the remaining pieces of denim and batting, which will make the pot holder top.

16 Place the quilted pot holder bottom on your work space. If you are right-handed, place it down so that you can put your right hand on top of it and your thumb matches up with the thumb section. If you are left-handed, place it down so that you can put your left hand on top of it and your thumb matches up with the thumb section.

17 Place one layer of denim, right side down, on top of the quilted pot holder bottom. Add the remaining piece of batting, then finish with the last piece of denim, right side up.

18 Pin all layers together around the perimeter of the pot holder except the bottom (which is where your hand will go in). Then, sew all layers together using a ½" seam allowance, leaving the bottom open. • ▶

19 Since this is such a thick bunch of fabric and batting, you will want to trim away a little bit of the seam allowance and excess batting. Also be sure to snip the space between the thumb and the hand, cutting close to, but not through, the stitches. • ▶

20 Turn right side out.

Note: the following diagrams are for a right-handed person. Photo on page 100 shows finished pot holder for a left-handed person.

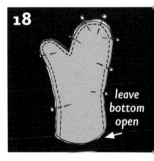

18 leave bottom open

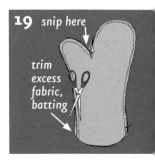

19 snip here

trim excess fabric, batting

103

Part 4: Finishing Touches

You'll use bias tape and stitching to make the raw edges at the bottom look nice. Bias tape will be used for the loop needed to hang your new holder.

21 Fold your bias tape in the middle lengthwise and sandwich the bottom layered raw edges of fabric and batting between the sides of the bias tape. • • • • • • • • • • • • • • • ▶

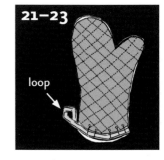

21–23

loop

22 Proceed around the opening of the pot holder, folding and sandwiching the layers of fabric, pinning as necessary to keep it in place.

23 Leave a loop of bias tape hanging when the bias tape reaches the side where you began. This will make the loop.

24 Sew in the bias tape, stitching close to the edge of the bias tape that is farthest from the fold.

25 Wrap it up pretty if it is a gift, or — if it is for you — pop it on and get cooking!

JEANS: THE ORIGINAL ITALIAN FASHION

The name "jeans" comes from the geographic origins of our favorite pants. Fashion historians have traced jeans back to the Italian city of Genoa, whose sailors wore heavy canvas trousers that were the earliest version of the jeans we know and love today. Over the years and through many languages, the proper noun Genoa, or adjective Genovese, became simply "jeans."

GET COMFY CUSHIONS

Do you ever wish you could just *live* in your oldest, most comfortable pair of jeans? Well, this project is the second best thing. Using your comfiest, but no longer wearable, fave pair of jeans, you'll make something you can live *with* 24/7: a plump, cozy cushion with fun bobble edging.

WHAT YOU'LL NEED:

* 2 jean legs
* 1 yard bobble edging
* 1 bag polyester stuffing

TIME

DIFFICULTY

PART 1: PLOTTING OUT YOUR PILLOW

You'll use your jean legs to create the pieces for the cushion front and back.

1 Cut one jean leg open at the outer seam. Cut off the hem and outer seam.

2 Measure the width of the open jean leg.

3 Cut the length of the jean leg so that it matches the width measurement found in step 2. Now, you should have a perfect square of jean. This is the cushion front. • • • • • • • • • • • • •▶

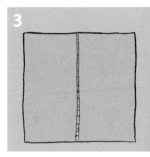

4 Cut apart the second jean leg at the outer seam. Cut off the hem and outer seam.

5 Place the cushion front on top of this jean leg and pin. (It doesn't matter here if right or wrong sides are together.) Cut around the cushion front to create another perfect square. Unpin the two pieces. Now you have a cushion front and a cushion back.

PART 2: FILLING OUT YOUR PILLOW

You will pin the trim to the front of the pillow, sew the pillow together, and stuff.

6 Lay the cushion front right side up on your work space. Pin the bobble edging around all four sides of the cushion front, matching the edge of the trim with the raw edges of the cushion front. The bobbles should point inward. • • • • • • • • • •▶

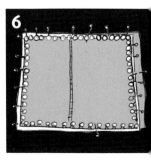

7 Place the cushion back, right side down, on top of the cushion front and bobble edging.

8 Pin all three layers together, careful not to catch any bobbles in the pins. • ▶

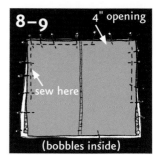

9 Carefully sew the layers together using a ¼" seam allowance and leaving a 4" opening in one side for turning and stuffing.

10 Clip corners and turn right side out.

11 Push stuffing in through the opening you left in the side until the cushion is nice and fat.

12 Pin the edges of the stuffing hole together, making sure that the bobble trim ribbon stays put between the layers of cushion front and back.

13 Sew the edges of the stuffing hole together close to the bobble trim.

14 Decorate as you like. Put your head on your pillow and have a nice long daydream!

BLUE JEANS: IT'S ALL ABOUT CHOICE

No wonder jean shopping can be overwhelming! As of 2006, there were more than 200 jean brands available in the United States — from expensive, international designers all the way down to dime-store brands.

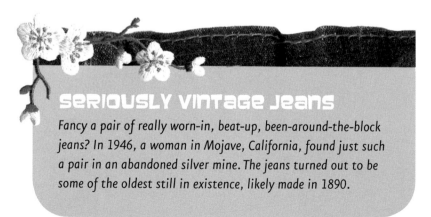

SERIOUSLY VINTAGE JEANS

Fancy a pair of really worn-in, beat-up, been-around-the-block jeans? In 1946, a woman in Mojave, California, found just such a pair in an abandoned silver mine. The jeans turned out to be some of the oldest still in existence, likely made in 1890.

BLue Jean BOOKWOrM BOOK Jacket

Is your favorite journal getting a bit beaten up? Do you feel shy when you are caught reading guilty-pleasure books with racy covers? If you answered yes to either of these questions, then this project is for you. With one jean leg, some ribbon, and a scrap of fashionable fabric, you can make an oh-so-classy book jacket from scratch. It even comes with a built-in bookmark and pocket for your pen.

WHAT YOU'LL NEED:

* 1 jean leg

* 1 ribbon, ¼" wide and long enough to go from the top of the book to the bottom, plus 2"

* 1 scrap alternate fashionable fabric (any type) at least 3" wide and 6" long

TIME ⏱ ⏱

DIFFICULTY

PART 1: GETTING READ-Y

You'll trace and cut out the shape of your book jacket.

1 Grab your jean leg. Cut off the hem to get one double-layered, rectangular piece of hemless jean. • • • • • • • • • • • • • • • ▶

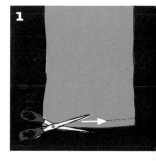

2 Place the double-layered rectangle of denim on your work space the long way (short edges at sides, long edges at top and bottom). Place an open book face up on top of the denim. Make sure the book is as flat as you can get it so you get a true measurement of its size. • • • • • • • • • • • • • • • • • • •

3 If your book fits on this rectangle with at least 2" to spare height wise, you can cut off the side seams of the jean leg and use one layer to make the book jacket. • • ▶

place book here and check for fit

If your book does not fit on the rectangle with at least 2" to spare height wise, you will need to cut the jean leg open along the inner seam to make a larger piece of jean fabric to work with. After doing this, align the intact outer seam in the center of this large piece of jean fabric with the book's spine, and use this entire piece of fabric.

4 Place your piece of jean fabric from step 3 wrong side up on the work space. Place your open book on top again, and trace around the edges of the open book.

5 Make a second outline, adding 1" to the top and bottom of your book outline (for the hem) and 4" on each side (for the flap pockets). Cut around this exterior line.

Part 2: Tying Up Loose Ends

Now you'll hem the top and the bottom of the book jacket, as well as the raw edge of the pockets, so that they don't fray.

6 Fold the top raw edge down ½" into the wrong side until the raw edge meets the top of the book outline. Pin in place and sew this fold down, using a ¼" seam allowance.

7 Repeat step 6 to hem the bottom of the book jacket.

8 Now you'll hem the raw edges of what will become the pockets. From each of the two remaining raw edges on the sides, draw one parallel line, 1" away from the raw edge.

9 Fold one short raw edge in ½" until it meets this line. Pin in place and sew, using a ¼" seam allowance. Repeat on the other short raw edge.

Part 3: Pocketing Away

You'll make the pockets into which you will slide the front and back covers of the book.

10 Fold in one of the hemmed short edges until the edge meets the outline of the book jacket. • • • • • • • • • • • • • • • •▶

11 Pin in place to create the pocket that you will slip the front cover of your book into.

12 Sew along the top and bottom of the pocket, leaving the middle open to slide in the book cover. Sew the pocket in place following the line of stitching that makes up the top hem and then along the stitching at the bottom hem. Repeat with the opposite side to make a pocket for the book's back flap.

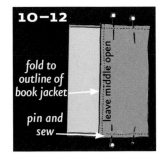

10–12

fold to outline of book jacket

pin and sew

leave middle open

PART 4: MAKING YOUR MARK

You'll sew a ribbon to the top of the jacket so that you'll never lose your place.

13 Fold the book jacket in half, right sides together, so that the two pocket edges meet. Locate the top of the book jacket, and make a mark right in the center.

14 Pin one end of ribbon into place on the mark you just made. Sew the ribbon end down with a few stitches. • • • • • • • • • • ▶

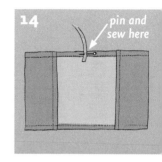

PART 5: A PLACE FOR PENS, TOO!

Here you will attach a pen holder to the book jacket.

15 Cut a piece of your fashionable fabric 5½"x 2".

16 Fold the long edges of this piece of fabric ½" to the wrong side, pin into place, and stitch close to the folds to create hems on both long sides. • • • • • • • • • • • • • • • • • ▶

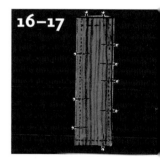

17 Fold the short edges ½" to the wrong side, pin into place, and stitch close to the folds to create hems on both short sides.

18 Position the fabric pen holder on the front of your denim book jacket. You can put the pen holder anywhere, as long as it does not overlap any of the flap pocket on the inside. Pin the pocket in place, then sew all but the top side to the denim, stitching along the existing hem lines. • • • • • • • • • • ▶

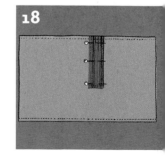

19 Slide in your book or journal and your pen, and head out to a café where you can read, write, or sketch!

KEY TO MY HEART KEY CHAIN

In a huge tote bag full of "necessities," important things like keys are often impossible to locate. This soft, plump key fob that wears its heart on its sleeve is the answer. Now you will always be able to dig out your keys—even if they have wiggled their way to the very bottom of your bag.

WHAT YOU'LL NEED:

* 1 scrap of jeans, approximately 4" × 4"

* 1 length of ribbon, 3" in length and approximately 1" wide

* small amount of polyester stuffing

TIME

DIFFICULTY

1 Fold your scrap of jeans in half and draw half a heart on it, starting at the fold, as you would when preparing to cut a paper valentine. Cut around your drawing and voilà, a jean heart! (You can also trace around a cookie cutter if you have little faith in your heart-drawing ability.) • • • • • • • • • • • • • • • • •▶

2 Pin this heart to another piece of jean scrap and cut around it to make a second heart.

3 Place one of your heart pieces right side up on your working space. Fold your length of ribbon in half and pin it anywhere on the side of your heart. Match up the raw edges of the ribbon with the raw edge of fabric, and make sure that the ribbon is inside the heart. • • • • • • • • • • • • • • • • •▶

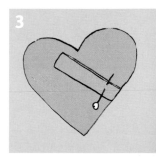

4 Place the second heart piece, right side down, on top of the first heart and ribbon. (Both right sides are together.)

5 Sew around the edges of the heart using a ¼" seam allowance and leaving a 1" opening in the side opposite from where the ribbon is pinned. Clip the corner at the bottom of the heart. •▶

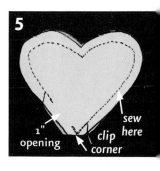

sew here

1" opening

clip corner

6 Turn the design right side out through the hole you left in the side.

7 Using the turning hole, fill with polyester stuffing.

8 When it is squishy enough to suit you, turn the raw edges of the hole inside the heart and pin closed.

9 Using a contrasting thread and a decorative stitch, sew around the heart close to the edge.

10 Hang your heart on your key chain and never lose your keys again!

Index